THEMES
for early years

SHAPES

D0417093

THEMES
for early years

Author Jenni Tavener

Editor Noel Pritchard

Assistant editor Joel Lane

Series designer Lynne Joesbury

Designer Toby Long

Illustrations Kim Woolley

Cover based on an illustration by Sue Coney

Action Rhymes, Poems and Stories compiled by Irene Yates

Songs compiled by Peter Morrell

Assemblies chapter by Barbara Zigliss

To Hannah, Christopher, Jonathan and Dominic

Designed using Adobe Pagemaker

Processed by Scholastic Limited, Leamington Spa

Published by Scholastic Limited, Villiers House, Clarendon Avenue, Leamington Spa, Warwickshire CV32 5PR

© 1995 Scholastic Limited   Text © 1995 Jenni Tavener
5 6 7 8 9 0   7 8 9 0 1 2 3 4

The publishers gratefully acknowledge permission to reproduce the following copyright material:
© 1993 Moira Andrew for 'Star shapes' from *Racing the Wind* by Moira Andrew (Nelson, 1993); © 1995 Debbie Campbell for 'Making shapes'; © 1993 Pie Corbett for 'A circle is . . .' from *Shapes* (OUP, 1993); © Pie Corbett for 'Curl and stretch' and 'My hand'; © 1995 John Foster for 'Drawing a square', 'Point with your finger', 'Roly poly plasticine', 'Squares' and 'What is a triangle?'; © 1995 Jean Gilbert for 'My balloon' and 'Shapes'; © 1994 Trevor Harvey for 'Stretch, curl and twist' from *Stretch, Curl and Twist* compiled by David Harmer (Collins Educational, 1994); © Trevor Harvey for 'Hall of mirrors' and 'People come in all shapes and sizes'; © 1995 Maggie Holmes for 'Pavement patterns'; © 1995 Karen King for 'Diana Diamond's tea party' and 'The strange thing in the wood'; © 1995 Trevor Millum for 'Allsorts' (words only); © 1995 Peter Morrell for 'The amazing maze'; © 1995 David Moses for 'Circle song'; © 1995 Judith Nicholls for 'Collage' and 'Scale tale'; © 1995 Gillian Parker for 'All sorts' (music only); © 1995 Irene Yates for 'The new baby' and 'The parcel surprise'; © 1995 Barbara Zigliss for 'Assembly on body shapes', 'Assembly on shapes in nature' and 'Assembly on regular shapes'.
Every effort has been made to trace copyright holders and the publishers apologise for any inadvertent omissions.

British Library Cataloguing-in-Publication Data A catalogue record for this book is available from the British Library.

ISBN 0-590-53347-9

THEMES
for early years

CONTENTS

INTRODUCTION

This *Themes for Early Years* book focuses on the topic of Shapes. It aims to provide early years educators with a comprehensive range of activities and support material to enable their pupils to explore the theme of Shapes in an interesting and informative way.

The book aims to offer teachers and adults supervising children aged three to six with a clear and flexible format of ideas which can be developed to create an integrated project on Shapes. Suggestions outlined in the Discussion and Follow-up sections can be used to adapt or extend the activities further so as to meet the particular needs of the children.

A topic on Shapes can stimulate children's enthusiasm for investigating their immediate environment, and offers a range of opportunities to develop an awareness of patterns and structures in the natural and man-made worlds. Overall, the book aims to create an exciting and positive insight into integrated topic work and to inspire a project investigating all aspects of shapes.

USING THEMES

The educational opportunities we provide for young children should lay the foundation for all future learning; but how can we use a theme-based approach to help achieve this?

The theme of Shapes encompasses many aspects of the world around us and links easily with other topic areas. In investigating shapes and their properties, children will also develop a greater awareness of their local environment. The chapters in this book deal with Shapes in nature (Chapter 1),

Symmetry and reflection (Chapter 2), Circles and spirals (Chapter 3), Three-dimensional shapes (Chapter 4), Patterns (Chapter 5) and Rectangles and triangles (Chapter 6). In all of the chapters in this book, children are encouraged to discover more about themselves and the world around them by looking at their families and friends, their own educational environment and the local community.

Theme-based work helps to provide a relevant and interesting learning environment for young children. Every child has a contribution to make, as shapes represent an integral part of their life; and as their awareness of their environment grows, they will develop attitudes and skills that will be important for future success in primary school.

Motivation is often a key to learning and helps to promote positive attitudes. Topic work can help to motivate children, as it provides an opportunity for them to contribute their own experiences, views and ideas on a shared theme. If children are interested in a topic and feel that the work is relevant to them, their enthusiasm and enjoyment will be all the greater.

Topic work also provides an ideal opportunity to develop social skills as the majority of the activities require children to work together. They will need to cooperate to carry out the activities successfully; and in group discussions, they will learn that everyone has an important contribution to make, both in intellectual and in practical terms.

Topic work can therefore be a valuable vehicle for encouraging children to work, play, talk, listen and respond to each other appropriately.

HOW TO USE THIS BOOK

This book offers a range of ideas which are intended to extend and develop learning skills through a shared topic on Shapes. It also aims to illustrate how learning opportunities can be developed through a cross-curricular approach. The length of time spent on the topic will greatly depend upon the response of the children. Very young children may only be able to sustain interest and enthusiasm in a topic for a short period; but by dividing the topic into shorter sub-themes, the children's natural curiosity can easily be rekindled as each new aspect of the topic is introduced.

TEACHING STRATEGIES

The content of this book has been deliberately organised to allow flexibility of use. Some teachers will wish to use almost all of the material while others may find it a useful dip-in resource to supplement their own ideas. In either case, it is important to adapt activities and choose resources to suit the needs of the individual children in your early years setting.

Similarly, there is no need to tackle the aspects of the topic in exactly the same order as presented in the book; and the same applies to the activities within each chapter.

A brief summary of the structure of this book is given below.

TOPIC WEB

The topic web gives a clear guide to all the activities within the book. Each activity, together with its page number, is listed under the appropriate curriculum area.

ACTIVITY PAGES

There are six chapters of activities, each related to a different aspect of the theme of Shape. The activities each provide information under the following subheadings: Objective, Group size, What you need, Preparation, What to do, Discussion and Follow-up activities. Some of the activities relate specifically to one of the photocopiable activity sheets at the end of the book, while others relate to stories, songs, poems or rhymes provided in the Resources chapter. Cross-curricular and extension suggestions are given where appropriate.

DISPLAYS

The Displays chapter provides suggestions for four different display projects, each directly related to one of the activities within the book. Display 1 (page 60) relates to the 'Symmetry shape monster' activity on page 26, Display 2 (page 61) to 'Kites with tails' on page 55, Display 3 (page 62) to 'Concertina caterpillar on page 14 and Display 4 (page 63) to 'Shape puppet plays' on page 39.

Each display makes full use of the children's work, and suggestions are given for ways to

enhance the displays using appropriate artefacts, objects and books. The displays illustrate how work from different subject areas (writing, drawing, maths, science and so on) can be combined to create a cross-curricular exhibition of children's work. Suggestions are also made for 'interactive' labels providing questions to encourage problem-solving, mathematical and observation skills. Details relating to colour schemes and mounting techniques are also provided.

ASSEMBLIES

This chapter provides ideas for planning assemblies related to the theme of 'Shapes'. Each assembly has its own practical ideas on how the children can contribute, ways in which they can be encouraged to reflect on the theme they are covering and a suggested prayer and song.

RESOURCES SECTION

These chapters provide a selection of action rhymes, poems, songs, stories and assembly ideas relating to the theme of Shape. Many of these are related to the activities, providing further opportunities to enrich the children's educational experience.

All of the resources in these chapters are photocopiable.

PHOTOCOPIABLE ACTIVITY SHEETS

This chapter provides eight pages of photocopiable activities linked to specific activities earlier in the book. The tasks relate to maths, language, science and RE.

RECOMMENDED MATERIALS

This page provides a list of children's story books, information books, poetry, music, paintings and educational resources which may be useful for a topic on Shapes.

EXPRESSIVE ARTS

Planning towards the National Curriculum and the Scottish 5–14 National Guidelines.

PREPARING FOR PRIMARY SCHOOL

The learning environment for children who are preparing for the National Curriculum should be built upon the needs of the individual child. The encouragement of positive attitudes and an enthusiasm to learn are of fundamental importance. Opportunities for constructive play and discussion are also essential, as both of these areas provide an important vehicle for young children's learning.

Opportunities which stimulate and facilitate talk are provided within the discussion section of every activity. This section aims to prepare the children for the National Curriculum by encouraging the development of effective speaking and listening skills — for example, sharing views, expressing ideas, asking questions — and by encouraging the children to take turns and to listen to others.

The National Curriculum was established to standardise the subjects, and subject content, taught at all levels of a child's education. It is intended that any child will be able to go to school anywhere in the country and find the same areas of the curriculum being covered for the same amount of time every week. These subjects are: English, Mathematics, Science, History, Geography, Design and Technology, Information Technology, RE, Art, Music and PE.

Most of the activities suggested in this topic are based on common play activities such as role-play, drawing, using construction toys or making puppets. However, each activity also has the specific objective of developing important skills in preparation for the first stage of the National Curriculum.

TOWARDS LEVEL ONE

National Curriculum learning requirements do not apply until children reach the age of five. The National Curriculum programmes of study were therefore written to suit the abilities of children who have reached their fifth birthday and who, depending on the part of the country in which they live, have spent anything from a term to a year in Reception class. The National Curriculum provides an overall programme of study for each subject, and asks teachers to assess the level of attainment of each child in the country when they reach Year Two. This assessment is carried out partly through nationwide testing; but for the most part, it is left to the teacher's professional judgement to allocate an overall level to each child.

Topic-based activities provide an ideal opportunity to maintain continuity and progression by enabling cross-curricular links to be made between different subject areas. For planning purposes, each activity in this book focuses on one of the subject areas detailed in the National Curriculum for Key Stage 1; several activities are also related to RE. These are outlined on the topic web on pages 8 and 9.

THE SCOTTISH NATIONAL GUIDELINES 5–14

In Scotland, there are National Guidelines for schools on what should be taught to children between the ages of five and fourteen. These National Guidelines are divided into six main curriculum areas: English Language, Mathematics, Environmental studies, Expressive arts, Religious and moral education and lastly Personal and social development.

Within these main areas further subjects are found: for example, 'Expressive arts' includes art and design, drama, music and PE. Strands are also identified within each subject: for example, Mathematics includes Problem-solving and enquiry and Shape, position and movement.

Most nurseries will find that the experiences they are offering children will provide a good foundation for this curriculum. The activities in this book have been specially written to prepare the children for many aspects of it, and they will also fit well into the pre-five curriculum guidelines issued by local authorities throughout Scotland.

Further issues regarding areas such as the hidden curriculum and child development are also addressed throughout the book.

CHAPTER 1
SHAPES IN NATURE

This chapter aims to encourage children to develop an appreciation of nature, and an awareness of the variety of shapes that can be found in the natural environment, by observing and investigating.

A COUNTRY DIARY

Objective

Geography – To increase awareness of the wide range of shapes which occur in the natural environment. To compile a diary of children's work based on information collected during a nature walk.

Group size

Any size.

What you need

A safe and secure outdoor area which features an interesting variety of plants and minibeasts, a copy of *The Country Diary of an Edwardian Lady* by Edith Holden (or a similar book containing illustrations of plants and animals), pencils, paper, card, a clipboard, hand-lenses, a stapler.

Preparation

Show the children *The Country Diary of an Edwardian Lady* or a similar book. Explain that the illustrations are drawings of real plants and animals found in nature.

What to do

Take the children on a nature walk and encourage them to watch out for interesting shapes which exist naturally outdoors. Point out features such as gnarled and twisted logs, spiral shells on snails, delicate circles and florets of lichen, sharp thorns in hedgerows, intricate spiders' webs and so on. Provide hand-lenses for close observation.

During the walk, invite each child to select one or more features to draw *'in situ'*. Once inside, encourage the children to write a short sentence about their picture; or an adult could act as scribe. Help the children to collage all the observational drawings and writings to make the pages of a 'Nature Diary' about their walk. Staple these pages together and add a card cover. Invite the children to think of a title to put on the cover of their diary, for example 'A Country Diary of Shapes in Nature'.

Discussion

Talk with the children about their experiences during the walk. Ask them to recall what they saw and to describe their favourite aspects of the walk. Encourage the children to talk about the observational drawings in their diary. Help them find out the names of some of the plants and animals, using reference books.

Follow-up activities

✧ Organise follow-up walks in the same area so that the children can collect further information for their diary about shapes in nature – for example, leaf and bark rubbings, photographs and samples of flowers, grasses and leaves to press.
✧ Involve the children in creating a large collage depicting an imaginary walk or garden. Encourage them to design their own flowers, birds and trees in a variety of unusual shapes, colours and sizes.

ACTIVITIES

HELPING HAND CALENDAR

Objective

RE – To promote an awareness of the importance of helping others. To make a calendar gift to reinforce the theme of helping others.

Group size

The whole group can join in with saying the rhyme. Ideally, the hand printing will be supervised on a one-to-one basis (if possible, ask a parent to help supervise the hand-printing stage).

What you need

A4 paper, coloured card (slightly bigger than A4), paint, pens, a small loose-leaf calendar (see illustration) for each child, adhesive, a hole punch, ribbon, sheets of newspaper, shallow containers, a sponge (big enough to fit a child's handspan), aprons, hand-washing facilities.

Preparation

To introduce the theme, read the following poem to the children:

Here are little hands to help you
Here are little hands to play
Here are little hands to hug you
Every single day.

Encourage the children to join in with the words and ask them to make up some finger actions to accompany the rhyme.

Then try replacing the word 'little' with a child's name. For example:

Here are Emma's hands to help you
Here are Emma's hands to play
Here are Emma's hands to hug you
Every single day.

Prepare the resources for the hand-printing stage by mixing powder paint to a thick consistency and then pouring it on to a sponge placed inside a shallow container. Cover a table surface with newspaper to protect it from the paint, and ensure that hand-washing facilities are nearby.

What to do

Tell the children they are going to make a calendar gift for someone whom they enjoy helping or hugging every day of the year. Provide each child with a template similar to the illustration above, and help them to use the hand-printing resources to make a print of both hands in the space at the centre of the rhyme. Remind the children to wash their hands straight away afterwards.

When the hand prints are dry, help the children to mount their work on coloured card and to add a small calendar to the bottom edge of their print. If you have a hole punch which is safe for children to use, let them make two holes along the top edge of their work, through which they can thread a piece of ribbon to hang up their calendar.

When finished, the children can give their 'helping hands calendar' to someone special.

Discussion

Ask the children to interpret the meaning of the rhyme in their own words. Focus their attention on the phrase 'hands to help you'. Ask how they can use their hands to help someone at home, at school or in the playground. Talk about who they can help: their parents, baby brothers/sisters and so on. Discuss what tasks their hands could do to be helpful: tidy their bedroom, pick up litter, comfort a friend.

Let the children share experiences of times when they helped someone or when someone helped them.

FRUITS AND VEGETABLES

Objective

Art — To examine a wide variety of different-shaped fruits and vegetables and to explore the differences by means of clay or dough modelling.

Group size

Individuals or small groups.

What you need

A selection of different-shaped fruits and vegetables (such as potatoes, carrots, bananas, pears, starfruit, rhubarb), soft pliable clay or dough (divided into balls about the size of an adult's fist), clay boards, hand-washing facilities, aprons.

Preparation

Encourage the children to identify and name the different fruits and vegetables. Talk about the different shapes and textures that can be seen: round, long, grooved, smooth, straight, bent and so on.

Read the poem 'Roly Poly Plasticine' in the Resources section on page 68.

What to do

Let the children handle the fruit and vegetables and compare the different shapes and sizes. Encourage them to describe the shapes from visual and tactile observation. Invite the children to manipulate the clay or dough to create their own representations of the fruit and vegetables. Display the real fruit and vegetables nearby, so that the children can easily remind themselves of the shapes. When the children have finished, let the models dry out before painting and varnishing them.

Discussion

Discuss the attributes of the foods. What do they feel like? Smell like? Taste like?

Talk with the children about how the fruit and vegetables grow. Which items grow on trees? Which grow underground? Discuss the names of the places where you can buy fruit and vegetables, such as a greengrocer's, farm shop, supermarket.

Follow-up activities

✧ Convert the structured play area into a 'greengrocer's shop' and invite the children to display their clay or dough produce.

✧ Explain to the children that they need to decide some things about their 'greengrocer's'. Where will the goods be displayed? Where will the shopkeeper stand? Should the customers be able to weigh the items themselves? Where should the money be kept? Ask them to add price tags, labels and signs to the shop — such as 'fresh produce', 'half price', 'open', 'closed', 'welcome', 'two for the price of one', and so on.

✧ Stimulate the children to draw or paint large posters advertising their greengrocer's shop.

✧ Challenge the children to design and make a container big enough to fit four apples in (for example), or strong enough to hold two pineapples.

CONCERTINA CATERPILLAR

Objective

Technology – To examine the changing shape of a caterpillar as it moves. To interpret these findings through simple technology.

Group size

Individuals or small groups.

What you need

An outdoor area where caterpillars can be seen in their natural habitat. Coloured strips of paper (approx. size 5cm x 60cm), adhesive, pens, scissors, magnispectors, hand-lenses, a ruler, circles of card (approx. 6cm in diameter).

Preparation

Take the children outside to view caterpillars in their natural environment. Invite them to use their hand-lenses, magnispectors and magnifying glasses for close observation of the caterpillars. Do not remove the caterpillars from their natural habitat.

What to do

Invite the children to construct a 'concertina caterpillar'. Provide each child with two strips of coloured paper. Help them to stick the two strips of paper together at right angles, as shown in Figure 1. Then show them how to fold the two strips by alternately folding the strips on top of each other, as shown in Figures 2 and 3. When the children have completed folding their paper, help them to glue the two loose ends together.

Suggest that they draw an imaginary caterpillar's 'face' on to a circle of card and then secure it to one end of their folded strip, thus completing their 'concertina caterpillar'.

Discussion

Encourage the children to describe, in their own words and actions, how a real caterpillar moves and how the shape of its body changes as it moves. Talk about how the concertina caterpillars move. Ask the children to think of other ways to make a model caterpillar.

Invite the children to look carefully at the leaves on which the caterpillars live. Talk about how the shapes of the leaves change as they are gradually eaten by the caterpillars.

Follow-up activities

✧ Read *The Very Hungry Caterpillar* by Eric Carle. Encourage the children to paint their own 'hungry caterpillar' and 'beautiful butterfly'. Use the paintings to highlight the differences in shape between the two animals.

✧ Provide fabric paints and a variety of different-shaped objects for printing. Encourage the children to design fabric butterflies to hang from the ceiling.

✧ Help the children to fold and cut sheets of plain paper to create symmetrical butterflies. Invite them to decorate their shapes using fluorescent paints or sticky paper, marbling inks, oil pastels, shiny paper or wax resist.

✧ Encourage the children to write their own version of the 'Very Hungry Caterpillar' story. Let them include all their own favourite foods for the caterpillar to eat. Use a hole punch to make a hole through all the pages in their book. Invite them to cut out a small caterpillar from felt and attach it to a length of wool. The caterpillar can then be pulled through each page of the book as it is read.

✧ Help the children to set up a vivarium containing caterpillars and leaves, for observational drawings and writing. Make sure you return the caterpillars to their natural habitat afterwards.

✧ Encourage the children to roll small balls of clay into caterpillar shapes. When the clay is dry, let them paint and varnish their caterpillars. Help each child to cut a leaf shape from green felt for their caterpillar to sit on.

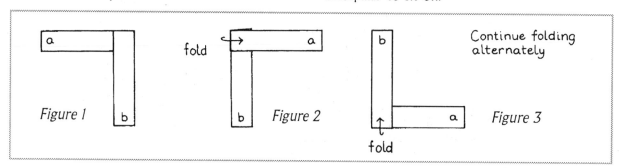

BODY BOOK

Objective

Science – To encourage a greater awareness of the shape of the human body.

Group size

Individuals or small groups.

What you need

A copy of photocopiable pages 88 and 89 for each child, pencils, crayons, adhesive, a mirror.

Preparation

You will need to prepare an A5 booklet for each child. This can be made by photocopying pages 88 and 89, then sticking the sheets back to back. Fold across the middle to create an A5 booklet.

Encourage the children to look at the shape and size of their hands, letting them compare their hands with their friends' and the teacher's. Can they identify similarities and differences between their hands and their feet? Ask them to name and identify features such as toes, nails, heel, sole, palm, fingers, span.

What to do

Provide each child with a booklet and invite them to write their name on the front. They can now record the shapes of their hands and feet in their own booklet by carefully drawing around them on the appropriate pages.

Invite the children to complete their 'Body book' by drawing a picture of themselves on the final page. Provide a full-length mirror to help them observe the shape of their body. Use the mirror to stimulate their awareness of body proportions, such as the length of their arms in relation to their body.

Discussion

Talk with the children about how the shape of their body can change as they bend and move their joints. Help them to identify and name their joints: ankle, elbow, knuckles, and so on.

If possible, invite a parent to bring their baby into the class or nursery. The children will enjoy watching it move, crawl and play. Use this experience to stimulate discussion about how the shape of their body has changed since they were a baby.

Follow-up activities

✧ During movement sessions, encourage the children to think of interesting shapes they can make with their whole body (round shapes, long shapes, flat shapes). Provide music for them to listen and move to – such as slow, gentle music to stimulate swirling, twisting shapes or music with a heavy rhythmic beat to inspire large, spiky shapes.
✧ Read the poem 'Curl and stretch' in the Resources section on page 70.
✧ Encourage the children to paint pictures of themselves dancing.

GROWTH OF A PLANT

Objective

History — To observe, and make a complete historical record of, the life of a plant.

Group size

A small group of children is appropriate for the planting stage of this activity. Subsequent activities which involve ongoing observation and monitoring can be planned for individuals, small groups or large groups.

What you need

Plant seeds such as sunflower seeds or beans, small pots (each labelled with the name of a child in the group), compost, a jug of water, shallow trays, a small trowel, a sunny window-sill, pens and paper, wool, scissors, clear adhesive film, a camera (optional).

Preparation

Tell the children to fill their small pot almost to the top with compost, and then to press a seed or bean gently into the soil. Each child can then water their pot and place it in a shallow tray on a sunny window-sill. Keep a jug of water nearby and urge the children to keep the compost moist. Check the pots daily, as the shoots will soon begin to show.

What to do

Compiling a 'growth book' as an ongoing record of the changes which happen to the plants from the first shoot through to maturity is an interesting project. The children can add three or four pieces of information to their book each week:
✧ a drawing of their plant
✧ a photograph (optional)
✧ a measurement (or piece of wool cut to the same length as the plant's height).

✧ a leaf (this should be sealed under adhesive film to prevent it from drying out).

The book can be used as a constant reminder of the subtle changes in the growth and shape of the plant as time goes by.

Discussion

As the plants begin to grow, encourage the children to observe and describe the shapes of the shoots, stems and developing leaves and flowers. They can go on to describe the feel of the plants, the smell and the colours.

During the growth stages, ask the children to predict what might happen next — for example, when flower buds begin to appear, or when the flowers have passed their best and begin to die.

Follow-up activities

✧ When the project is over, encourage the children to look back at the photographs and pictures to remind themselves about the various stages of development and growth.
✧ Read the story 'The Parcel Surprise' in the Resources section on page 85.
✧ Read the story 'Jack and the Beanstalk'.
✧ Encourage the children to work together to paint a giant beanstalk that can be displayed up the wall and even along the ceiling.
✧ Convert the structured play area into a flower shop or garden centre.

SORTING NATURAL OBJECTS

Objective

Maths — To reinforce sorting, matching and set-making skills and to develop mathematical language.

Group size

Individuals or small groups.

What you need

A collection of natural objects (such as shells, cones, seeds, flowers, feathers, conkers, stones, fruits and vegetables), small PE hoops, a collection of empty containers such as old ice-cream tubs, a large shallow tray.

Preparation

Let the children help to lay out the selection of natural objects on the large shallow tray. Discuss the different attributes of the various objects and prompt the children to think about how they can be grouped. Involve them in practical set-making by either asking them to make their own set, such as a set of objects which come from trees, or giving them a set to identify (explain that more than one phrase may describe this set correctly).

What to do

Encourage the children to use the PE hoops for two-way sorting, i.e. practical Venn diagrams. Choose two unrelated criteria relevant to your collection, for example round objects and edible objects. Then ask the children to place all of the round objects into one hoop to make a 'set of round objects' and all of the edible objects into the second hoop to make a 'set of edible objects'.

Cross the two hoops over as shown in Figure 1, and ask the children to identify those objects which match both criteria: round, edible objects. Tell them to place this set of objects in the appropriate area of the hoops, as shown in Figure 2.

Children can record their practical work by drawing a picture of their Venn diagram on a large sheet of paper. Help them to label each set, or scribe the words for them.

Discussion

Talk with the children about the wide variety of shapes, patterns and textures which can be found in this collection.

Discuss where the natural objects originated from — feathers come from birds, conkers from trees. Talk about the meanings of the terms *natural* and *man-made*.

Follow-up activities

✧ Use the natural objects for observational drawings or paintings.
✧ Children can use the feathers, shells, seeds and other objects to construct a two-dimensional collage.
✧ Encourage the children to create a three-dimensional collage by using the assortment of natural objects to decorate a solid shape made from Plasticine, play dough or clay.
✧ Set up a display contrasting natural objects with man-made objects. Use this as an interactive display for sorting and matching tasks.
✧ Use the PE hoops to introduce 'three-way sorting' of natural and man-made objects.

Figure 1

Place one PE hoop over the other

Figure 2

round objects   edible objects

(pebble, conker)   (banana, celery)

round edible objects (orange, grapefruit)

FLOWER POEMS

Objective

English — To inspire descriptive and poetic language.

Group size

Individuals or small groups.

What you need

A variety of real flowers and/or plants in unbreakable containers (be aware of plants which should not be handled), a thick marker pen, circles of coloured card or paper, hand-lenses or magnifying glasses.

Preparation

Encourage the children to examine the flowers, using the magnifying glasses to look carefully at the intricate shapes and details of the individual petals, buds and flower centres. Suggest they touch the flowers to compare the various textures.

What to do

Ask the children to describe the plants and flowers in their own words. Record the descriptive words and phrases used by the children on coloured circles of card or paper. Inspire poetic use of language by inviting the children to arrange these words and phrases as flower petals around a circular card on which the rhyme 'Flower, flower in front of me, what lovely things I can see' has been written. Display the resulting flower poems on the wall, as a mobile or in a group poem book. (See illustration.)

Discussion

Talk with the children about the different parts of the plants; encourage them to identify and name features such as leaves, stems, petals and veins. Discuss the shapes and colours of these parts.

Talk about what things plants need to keep healthy, such as light and water. Let the children say which flowers are their favourites. What are the reasons for their choices?

Follow-up activities

✧ Encourage the children to make comparisons between two different plants, using comparative vocabulary such as *bigger, the same as, smaller than.*
✧ The children could make observational drawings or paintings of the plants and flowers.
✧ Use the leaves of plants or trees for printing. Compare the shapes and patterns printed by these different leaves.

CHAPTER 2
SYMMETRY AND REFLECTION

Learning to understand how symmetry and reflections work will help in the development of children's overall awareness of shapes. All children enjoy experimenting with mirrors and reflections and this enthusiasm can be used to focus their attention on symmetry and the properties of shapes.

SPOON REFLECTIONS

Objective

Science — To investigate how the shape of the 'mirror' changes the appearance of the reflection.

Group size

Individuals or small groups.

What you need

Clean shiny spoons, reflective paper, scissors, small mirrors, paper cut to the shape of a spoon outline (approx. size A4), pens, pencils.

Preparation

Provide the children with the shiny spoons and a mirror. First of all, ask them to look at their reflection in the mirror. Then let them explore how the appearance of their face changes when reflected in the spoons. How does the shape of their face change when they look in the front and the back of the spoon? Can the children describe these changes in their own words? Challenge them to investigate which side of the spoon gives an upside-down reflection. Can they make their reflection turn the right way up by twisting the spoon around (without turning it over)? What happens when they bring the spoon close up to their face? What happens when they move the spoon away again?

What to do

Provide each child with two pieces of paper cut into the shape of a spoon. Suggest that they use one piece to draw the reflection of their face while looking in the front of their spoon, and use the

second piece to draw a picture of their reflection while looking in the back of the spoon.

When everyone has finished, mount the 'spoon' pictures back to back on shiny paper and then display them as a mobile or use them to make a spoon-shaped book.

Discussion

Encourage the children to discuss their feelings. Were any of the reflections a surprise? Did they expect to see themselves upside-down? Ask them if they would like to have a curved mirror instead of a flat mirror in their bedroom or bathroom. Can they give reasons for their choice?

Follow-up activities

✧ Say the poem 'Hall of Mirrors' in the Resources section on page 74.
✧ Provide a variety of other shiny objects with curved surfaces, so that the children can experiment with looking at their reflections. Ask them to find out which objects make them appear upside-down.
✧ Introduce the terms 'convex' and 'concave'.

THREE BEARS CARD GAME

Objective

English – To introduce the children to the language of symmetry and reflection through playing a card game.

Group size

Two to four children.

What you need

A copy of photocopiable page 90, coloured pens, pencils, scissors.

Preparation

Read the story 'Goldilocks and the Three Bears' to the children. Provide each group with a copy of photocopiable page 90 depicting the characters of Goldilocks and the Three Bears, then encourage the children to colour in the pictures symmetrically.

When they have completed the colouring, help them to cut each picture in half along the dotted line.

What to do

Use the set of pictures to play the following sorting and matching game for two players.

Divide the cards into two sets: one set containing the right-hand sides of the pictures, the other set containing the left-hand sides. Share one of the sets out between the players.

Lay the other set face down in front of the players, who then take turns to turn over one card at a time. The players may keep cards that match the pictures on the cards in their set, and must replace those that do not match. The first player to match all of her cards is the winner.

Discussion

Talk about words and phrases that can be used in place of the terms *symmetry* and *symmetrical*: 'the same as', 'similar', 'matching', 'pairs', 'alike', 'reflection', 'double'.

Provide each child with a small mirror and show them how to hold it along the dotted line on their Three Bears picture, to help them understand the terms *mirror image* and *reflection*.

Follow-up activities

✧ Let the children use their pictures to retell the story of Goldilocks and the Three Bears and record their own version in spoken words, pictures or writing.

✧ Encourage the children to write a 'pretend' letter from Goldilocks to the Three Bears, telling them that she was sorry for eating their porridge and breaking their chair.

'FUNNY FACE' MIRROR BOOKS

Objective

RE – To help children gain a greater awareness of their feelings and the feelings of others.

Group size

Individuals or small groups.

What you need

Small hand-mirrors (or mirror card), A4 card, pens, pencils, coloured magazines or comics, adhesive, scissors, aprons.

Preparation

Ask the children to look at their face in a mirror and discuss the main features of it. Talk about how the shape of their features changes as their mood changes. Encourage them to look in the mirror while imitating the shape of a sad face. Can they think of other expressions to imitate? Talk with the children about how they feel when they see a friend, teacher or parent smiling or frowning. Which expression do they prefer? Encourage them to share their own views about how they can use their face to make other people feel happy, for example by offering a smile or making them laugh.

What to do

Tell the children they are going to use their mirror to create a 'funny faces' mirror book, to be used for making themselves or others laugh if they need cheering up. To do this, provide each child with a piece of folded A4 card and help them to stick their mirror into the middle section of the card.

Next, encourage the children to fill the sections on either side with 'funny' pictures cut out of magazines and comics. They could also include drawings of themselves or their friends pulling funny faces, if they wish. Alternatively, encourage them to create some 'funny-shaped characters' by cutting out several different pictures from magazines or comics and then dividing these into separate sections – legs, head, body and so on. The children can then mix and match these separate pieces to create original and amusing pictures.

As another alternative, the children could think of their own ideas for pictures which make them laugh or smile.

Discussion

Talk with the children about what makes them feel happy, sad, excited, frightened and so on. How can they help make other people feel happy?

Follow-up activities

✧ Say the poem 'Hall of Mirrors' from the Resources section on page 74.
✧ Encourage the children to paint pictures of happy faces.
✧ The children can make 'happy face' badges by drawing a smiling face on to a circle and then sticking Velcro to the back.
✧ Help the children to decorate plain biscuits by adding a 'smiley face' with icing.
✧ The children can make a 'smiley face' flag by drawing the picture on a sheet of plain fabric using fabric crayons, before securing it to a length of dowelling or garden cane.

REFLECTING A TUNE

Objective

Music – To inspire the children's sense of beat and rhythm. To develop listening skills by playing and 'echoing' short tunes.

Group size

Any size.

What you need

A selection of percussion instruments such as drums, tambourines, triangles, wood blocks, bells, maracas and so on (if possible, provide one instrument for each child), a comfortable place to sit.

Preparation

Encourage the children to take turns to clap the rhythm of their own name. For example, 'Tim' would involve a single clap; 'Timmy' would involve two claps, one for each syllable; 'Timothy' would therefore need three claps.

What to do

Ask the children to sit in a circle, making sure that each child is comfortable and that they can see easily. Provide yourself and each child with a percussion instrument, then play a musical game with the children by tapping several short rhythms for them to 'echo' using their instrument.

As the children gain confidence, ask them to take turns making up short tunes of three or four beats for the rest of the group to repeat or 'echo'.

Discussion

Talk with the children about the different words they can use to describe 'echoing' or 'repeating' a tune, such as 'reflecting', 'copying' or 'following'. Encourage them to think of their own descriptions.

Talk about the different sounds that each instrument makes. Which instruments make little sounds and which make big ones?

Look at the different shapes of the instruments. Count how many round instruments you have, how many triangle-shaped ones, and so on.

Follow-up activities

✧ The children can play their instruments while singing popular nursery rhymes or songs.

✧ Ask the children to work in pairs to make up short tunes, using more than one instrument. Can they make up words to go with their tunes?

✧ Provide a tape recorder to record the children's music and songs.

✧ Set up an interactive music display. To do this, record the sound of each instrument on tape, then display this tape alongside the real instruments. Invite the children to listen to the recordings. Can they match the correct instruments to the sounds on the tape? Suggest that they play the instruments one at a time to help find the answers.

SYMMETRICAL BUTTON BADGES

Objective

Technology – To gain a practical understanding of symmetry and to develop creative design skills. To provide the children with an opportunity to make something that can be used.

Group size

Small groups.

What you need

Buttons (in a variety of interesting shapes, sizes and colours), card, adhesive, adhesive tape, a mirror, scissors, pens and pencils, small containers, Velcro.

Preparation

Cut the card into small rectangles, triangles or circles (approx. size 8cm²). Check that you have more than one button in each style. Cover a table with a cloth or newspaper to protect it from the adhesive.

What to do

Provide each child with a selection of buttons and some small containers into which to sort them. Ask them to start by sorting the buttons into matching pairs or sets, as these will be needed to create symmetrical patterns. Any 'odd' buttons can then be placed in a separate container and used as centre-pieces on the badge (see Figure 1).

Let each child select one of the card shapes; then invite them to design their badge by arranging several buttons on their piece of card to make a symmetrical pattern. Before sticking the buttons in place, encourage the children to use a mirror to check that their design is symmetrical. If it is not, suggest that they rearrange their design and then check again before sticking.

When the adhesive is dry, invite the children to decorate the spaces in between the buttons with felt-tipped pens or pencils. Remind them that the colours and patterns should also be applied symmetrically. Alternatively, some children may wish to cut around the buttons to create a totally new shape.

Finally, help the children to tape a piece of Velcro on to the back of each badge. The children can wear their badges or display them in a class 'jeweller's window'.

Discussion

Talk with the children about other symmetrical items that we wear. Are their trousers symmetrical? What about their jumpers, shoes or socks?

Discuss with children how to turn the structured play area into a 'Class Jeweller's'. What will they need? How can they make the jeweller's shop look attractive? Talk about the signs and labels they might need. Discuss how they can make items of 'jewellery'. Will the shop have a watch mender? Where will the watch mender work? Where will the customers stand?

Figure 1

Follow-up activities

✧ Say the poem 'Collage' in the Resources section on page 74.
✧ Provide the children with small shells, adhesive and card and let them construct symmetrical shell brooches.
✧ Provide beads, buttons or pasta shells and strong thread for the children to create symmetrical necklaces or bracelets. To do this, tie a knot in the centre of the thread, then ask the children to complete one half of the necklace. They can then complete the second half of the necklace by carefully following the same pattern of beads (see Figure 2).
✧ Invite the children to make a 'jewellery box' or small 'gift box' by decorating a small cardboard box with buttons. They can decorate the sides and lid of the box with symmetrical patterns.

Figure 2

SYMMETRICAL PATTERNS

Objective

Maths – To help the children gain an awareness of symmetrical patterns.

Group size

Individuals or small groups.

What you need

A copy of photocopiable page 91 for each child, pictures or photographs of butterflies, bendy straws, a selection of shapes cut from coloured adhesive paper (the variety and type of shapes will depend on the age and ability of the children), adhesive tape, scissors.

Preparation

Look at the photographs and pictures of butterflies. Talk about the symmetrical patterns on their wings.

What to do

Provide each child with a copy of photocopiable page 91 and a selection of coloured shapes. Encourage them to use their shapes to arrange a simple pattern on one wing (forewing plus hindwing) of the 'butterfly'. When they are happy with their design, they can stick the shapes in place.

Next, invite the children to select a matching set of coloured shapes. They can position these shapes on the other wing of their butterfly to form a symmetrical pattern or mirror image.

Help the children to cut around their butterfly and attach it to the short end of a bendy straw, as shown in Figure 1. When this is done, the children can 'flick' the straw to make their butterfly flap its 'wings'.

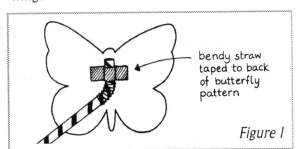

bendy straw taped to back of butterfly pattern

Figure 1

Discussion

Invite the children to talk about the patterns they have made. Can they identify and name the different shapes?

Can the children explain in their own words how they made their butterfly's wings flap?

Follow-up activities

Use the symmetrical butterflies on the bendy straws to create the following displays, which are both mathematically stimulating and pleasing to look at.

✧ *Make a mobile*

Fasten two to four butterflies on straws together by taping or stapling together the 'handle' ends of the straws. Attach a thread to the centre of each butterfly, and hang up the group to create an interesting mobile. Use the mobiles to pose questions, such as 'How many mobiles have three butterflies?', 'Which mobiles have six wings?', 'Calculate the number of butterflies on any two mobiles', and so on.

✧ *Make a three-dimensional display*

A dramatic effect is created if the butterflies are displayed against a dark background or a background scene of painted grass and flowers. Start off by cutting a sufficient number of small slits in the background material, and then attach the background to the display board. Now insert the long end of each bendy straw 'butterfly' into a slit on the background, creating a three-dimensional effect as the butterflies hover against the background scene.

MIRROR MIME

Objective

PE – To stimulate an interest in expressive mime or dance. To develop teamwork and co-operation skills. To help children listen and respond to instructions.

Group size

Any size.

What you need

A room with enough space for the children to move around freely and safely.

Preparation

Create a story entitled 'The Magical Mirror', about a child whose mirror image comes to life. Incorporate opportunities for the children to act out the part of the child or the mirror image. The following outline can be adapted and extended with the children's own ideas.

> 'Once upon a time, a child was very upset because he had not been invited to a friend's party. He sat at home in his bedroom feeling very lonely and miserable, and wishing that he had a friend to play with. He looked at himself in the mirror and wiped his tears away. Then he began to pull funny faces at himself in the mirror to cheer himself up.
>
> 'Then something very strange began to happen: The boy stepped to one side away from the mirror, and amazingly the mirror image copied him by stepping right out of the mirror. The boy could not believe it, so he stepped from side to side to see what would happen.'

What to do

Invite the children to re-enact the scenes from this story. Encourage them to work in pairs: one pretending to be the child, the other to be his mirror image. Let them begin by stepping from side to side, with one child mirroring the other.

Then continue the story:

> 'Next, the child lifted one arm and the image did the same. He lifted both arms and stepped forwards and backwards. Then he hopped, jumped and turned around.'

Encourage the children to repeat these actions in pairs, one child mirroring the other. Can they think of their own set of movements – for example, bending, twisting, moving fast or in slow motion? Let the children take it in turns to be the mirror image.

Explain that the boy was so happy that he started to dance. Let the pairs of children create a short simple dance of, say, three or four movements – for example, a jump, a hop, a nod of the head and a step to one side.

End the activity by explaining that the child was so tired, he fell asleep on his bedroom floor. Tell the children to finish their dance by lying down, still and quiet.

Provide opportunities for each pair to perform their dance or sequence in front of their peers.

Discussion

Ask the children to recall the events of the magical mirror story. Talk about what happened. The children can share their ideas about how they would feel if their mirror image jumped out at them. Encourage them to talk about their mime or dance sequence.

Follow-up activities

✧ As they become more proficient at 'mirroring' each other, stimulate their ideas further by introducing some music for them to move to. Extend this by asking them to work out a short 'mirror dance'.

✧ Ask the children to paint or draw a picture depicting a scene from the story.

✧ Introduce other stories which refer to 'magic mirrors', such as 'Snow White and the Seven Dwarfs' or 'Alice Through the Looking Glass'. Talk about the characters and plots in these stories. Encourage the children to re-enact favourite scenes from the stories – for example, the Queen from 'Snow White' calling 'Mirror, mirror on the wall, who is the fairest of them all?'

ACTIVITIES

SYMMETRY SHAPE MONSTER

Objective

Art – To provide the children with the opportunity to design and make their own toys, and to give practical reinforcement of their concepts of symmetry and symmetrical objects.

Group size

Individuals or small groups.

What you need

A selection of non-fraying fabric pieces (approx. size 30cm x 40cm), sewing thread, pins, needles, soft toy stuffing, small pieces of coloured felt, fabric scissors, pencils, fabric adhesive (such as Copydex), a pin cushion, symmetrical shapes cut from paper (approx. size 25cm x 35cm), a story about monsters such as *Not Now, Bernard* by David McKee or *Where the Wild Things Are* by Maurice Sendak (see Recommended materials list on page 96).

Preparation

Read a story such as *Not Now, Bernard* or *Where the Wild Things Are* to the children.

Ask them to identify and name the different paper shapes, then to select one of the shapes to use as a pattern for a 'monster toy'. Alternatively, allow them to make their own pattern by drawing a symmetrical shape on paper and cutting it out (approx. size 25cm x 35cm).

What to do

Help the children to pin their paper shape on to two pieces of non-fraying fabric and then cut out the two shapes from fabric to make the body. Help them to sew their fabric shapes together, leaving a gap through which to insert the stuffing. When the children have stuffed their shapes, help them to sew up the gap. Now suggest that they cut out small shapes from felt to represent the 'monster's' eyes, nose, mouth, fangs, hair and so on (see illustration). Secure these felt 'features' in place using fabric adhesive. Remind the children that the features need to be positioned symmetrically. When this is done, ask the children to think of a name for their 'symmetrical shape monster'.

Discussion

Ask the children to create an imaginary personality for their 'monster'. Can they give it a name? Where does it live? What does it eat? What sounds does it make?

Follow-up activities

✧ Use the monster toys to encourage imaginative play.
✧ Ask the children to write stories or descriptions of their toy. Provide them with writing paper which matches the shape of their monster (oval, triangle and so on).
✧ Use the toys for observational painting and drawing.
✧ Arrange a display to illustrate the various stages of work generated by the sewing activity: the paper patterns, the corresponding toys, the observational pictures, the stories and descriptions, and so on.

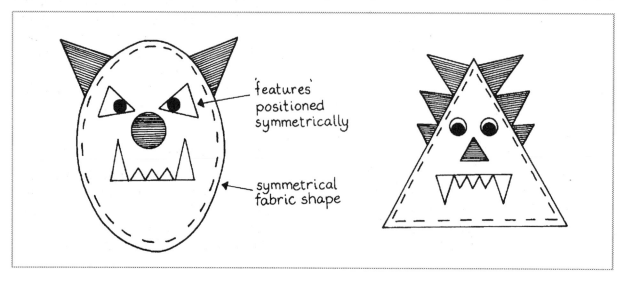

'features' positioned symmetrically

symmetrical fabric shape

CHAPTER 3
CIRCLES AND SPIRALS

The activities in this section look at circles and spirals in the world around us and focus on basic mapping skills, dance and movement, and on the importance of circles as cogs and wheels in machinery.

CIRCULAR ROUTES

Objective

Geography – To increase the children's awareness of how to follow a planned route using a map.

Group size

The activity can be adapted to suit small groups or large groups.

What you need

Paper, pens, pencils, scissors, adhesive, a large circle drawn on a sheet of paper or card (approx. size 50cm in diameter).

Preparation

Take the children on a circular walk around your building or grounds. Ask them to look out for 'landmarks' or 'points of interest' along the route.

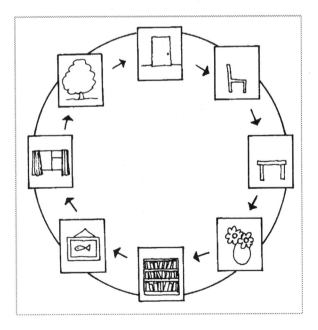

Repeat this walk a few times to familiarise the children with the route.

What to do

Encourage each child to draw one of the 'landmarks' or 'points of interest' seen on your circular walk. Help the children to glue their pictures on to the large circle, arranging them in the order in which they occur on the walk. To do this, choose any point on the circle to place the picture representing the first landmark (the place where you started your walk) and work forwards from there. Once everyone is happy with the order of the pictures, stick them in place.

Draw large arrows between each 'landmark' and the next to indicate the direction of your route (see illustration). Display the 'map' of your circular route on the wall and use it for discussion and follow-up activities.

Discussion

Look at the 'map' with the children and pose problem-solving questions, such as 'If I start at the "coat pegs" and follow the arrows, what will I see next?' or 'If I walk all the way round the route, how many of our "landmarks" will I see altogether?' Encourage the children to share views and ideas about their favourite 'landmarks' and 'points of interest' during the walk.

Discuss other routes which the children follow – for example, around a local park.

Follow-up activities

✧ Invite the children to draw or paint an imaginary circular route, and to add make-believe landmarks along this route. Their imaginary route could be based on a favourite story.

✧ Invite the children to draw their route to school.

PAINTING SPIRALS

Objective

Art – To increase awareness of spirals in natural and man-made objects. To explore spirals using paint.

Group size

Individuals or small groups.

What you need

Black and white paper (various sizes, large and small), black and white paint, painting equipment (include brushes of varying thicknesses), aprons, hand-washing facilities, a collection of spiral objects or objects with a spiral pattern – shells, springs, gift ribbon, ivy, bean stalks, pictures of helter-skelters or spiral staircases.

Preparation

Encourage the children to look carefully at the spirals in your collection of

pictures and objects. Pose questions such as 'Where does the spiral start and finish?' Let the children follow the spiral patterns with their finger. Invite them to draw spirals in the air, starting with small spirals (using their finger as an imaginary pen) and then moving on to large spirals (swinging their whole arm).

What to do

Provide the children with black and white paper, black and white paint and paintbrushes. Suggest that they paint white spirals on the black paper and black spirals on the white paper. Let them experiment with different methods of creating a spiral – for example, starting in the middle of the page and working outwards, or starting on the edge of the page and working inwards. Ask the children to create 'tiny' spirals and 'enormous' spirals using a variety of different-sized brushes.

When the paintings are dry, help the children to cut around the outside edge of each spiral. An interesting effect can be produced by displaying the spirals against a background of black and white panels or checks, as shown in the illustration. Alternatively, display the spirals in a group 'spiral book' or hang them from the ceiling as mobiles.

Discussion

Talk about the spiral objects in your collection. Can the children think of other spirals they have seen?

Ask the children questions about their paintings to help them develop an awareness of relative shape and size: 'Which size brush helped to make a big spiral?' and 'Which size brush helped to make a small spiral?'

Follow-up activities

✧ Show the children how to print spiral pictures. This can be done by gluing a coil of string on to a sheet of card or block of wood. Dab the string with paint and then print it on to paper or fabric.
✧ Encourage the children to make spiral decorations by cutting spirals of shiny paper to hang from the ceiling.
✧ Provide the children with clay, Plasticine or play dough to make models in coil and spiral shapes.
✧ Read the story 'The Strange Thing in the Wood' in the Resources section on page 83.

COMPOSING A SONG

Objective

English – To stimulate an interest in composing a 'new' version of the song 'The wheels on the bus'. To inspire co-operation and teamwork.

Group size

Small or large groups.

What you need

A copy of the song 'The wheels on the bus', pictures and photographs of vehicles, a safe area from which to view traffic (optional).

Preparation

Look at pictures of different vehicles, or take the children to a safe place from which to observe different modes of transport. Encourage the children to name and identify the vehicles they see. Sing the song 'The wheels on the bus'.

What to do

Ask the children to use their observations of vehicles to create a new version of the song 'The wheels on the bus'. First, ask them to decide what type of vehicle they would like to sing about – for example, taxi, train, bike, tractor, tram, lorry, coach, milk float and so on. Then encourage them to create the first verse by substituting their own choice of wheeled vehicle for the word 'bus'. For example, 'The wheels on the taxi . . .' Help the children to compose their second verse by asking them to think of a person who might be inside the vehicle they have chosen – for example, a tourist might be in a taxi.

Next, ask the children: 'What might this person be doing in the vehicle while riding along?' A tourist in a taxi, for example, might be looking at the view. Let the children have fun selecting a single word, sound or phrase which could be used in their song to describe these actions. The tourist, for example, could be saying 'Look'.

Finally, help the children to put these ideas together to create two original verses to their 'new' song:

> The wheels on the taxi go
> Round and round
> Round and round
> Round and round
> The wheels on the taxi go
> Round and round
> All day long.
>
> The tourist in the taxi says
> Look, look, look
> Look, look, look
> Look, look, look
> The tourist in the taxi says
> Look, look, look
> All day long.

Discussion

Invite the children to compose further verses featuring different characters and actions. Alternatively, invite them to compose another two-verse song about a different type of vehicle.

Follow-up activities

✧ Help the children to record their song using a tape recorder.
✧ Help the children to make a booklet containing the words to their new song. They can then decorate the cover to resemble the vehicle in their song. Card wheels can be added to the cover, using paper-fasteners to allow the wheels to spin.
✧ Display a collection of real wheels in the classroom for close observation. Include wheels of different sizes, such as toy wheels, pram wheels, a car tyre and so on.
✧ Invite the children to bring in toys with wheels.

THE SEASONAL CYCLE

Objective

Science — To help the children gain an awareness that the seasons rotate in a cycle. To construct a 'seasons wheel' to reinforce understanding.

Group size

Individuals or small groups.

What you need

Paper-fasteners, pens, pencils, pictures and photographs showing scenes of the four seasons, A4 sheets of card, circles of card (approx. size 20cm diameter).

Preparation

Can the children tell you what season it is? Talk about what can usually be seen at this time of year. Show the children the photographs and pictures of different seasons. Work together to sort the pictures into four groups — one for each of the seasons. Explain that the seasons rotate in the same order every year: spring, summer, autumn, winter. (To an adult, it may be clear that recent changes in the climate have affected the pattern of the seasons; but the basic sequence of four seasons remains the same.)

Cut the top right-hand quarter from each of the A4 sheets of card (Figure 1), and draw lines dividing the card circles into four sections (Figure 2).

What to do

Provide each child with a circle of card and invite them to draw a picture of one season in each section. Remind them to draw the seasons in the correct order. When this is done, help the children to pierce a hole through the centre of the card circle and A4 piece of card and then to fasten their circle on to the piece of card using a paper-fastener as shown in Figure 3. Let the children experiment with turning their wheel to reveal one season at a time within the cutout frame, to reinforce their awareness that the seasons form a continuing cycle year after year.

Discussion

Talk about events that recur throughout the year, such as birthdays, New Year, religious celebrations and so on, to reinforce the yearly cycle. Look at calendars and talk about the names of the days and months.

Follow-up activities

◇ Sing the 'Circle Song' in the Resources section on page 80.
◇ Invite the children to construct a wheel illustrating the various stages in the life-cycle of a frog or butterfly, or the seasonal cycle of a deciduous tree.
◇ Set up a nature table to display objects collected by the children that are specific to a particular season.
◇ Encourage the children to create seasonal observation pictures by allowing them to paint scenes outdoors or looking out through a window.

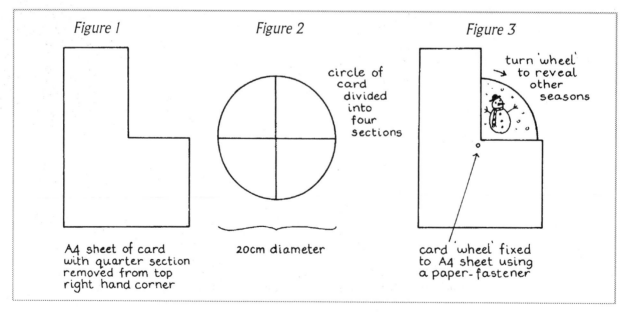

Figure 1

Figure 2

Figure 3

circle of card divided into four sections

turn 'wheel' to reveal other seasons

A4 sheet of card with quarter section removed from top right hand corner

20cm diameter

card 'wheel' fixed to A4 sheet using a paper-fastener

TOUCHING CIRCLES

Objective

Maths – An investigative activity to stimulate the children's interest in maths and to inspire their curiosity.

Group size

Individuals or small groups.

What you need

A set of at least seven circular objects all the same size (lids, templates, logic-block shapes) for each child, paper and pens, paints (optional).

Preparation

Ask the children to help gather the collection of circles, or to help make the circle templates from card.

What to do

Provide each child with a set of the circle shapes. Then ask them how many identical circles will fit around a single central circle. Explain that each circle should touch the edges of the neighbouring circles, as shown above. Encourage the children to compare their results. They will soon discover that the answer is always the same! The activity will show that six circles fit around the centre circle.

Ask children to test whether this is always true, using a set of larger circles and a set of smaller circles, and to draw around their circles to create patterns of 'touching circles'. They can then decorate their circles, using pens (or paints).

Discussion

Encourage the children to talk about their findings. Were they surprised at the results? Challenge them to predict what might happen with other shapes. For example, how many squares would fit around a square, or triangles around a triangle? Encourage the children to work together to find out the answers, and then to share ideas and discuss the outcomes with each other.

Follow-up activities

✧ Suggest that the children use the card/paper circles to make a flower display. Encourage them to decorate the circles with their own designs. They can then place their 'flowers' on a green 'grass' background and use paint, felt-tipped pens or coloured paper to add stalks or leaves to the display.

✧ Use the 'touching circles' idea to make three-dimensional flowers. To do this, help the children to stick yoghurt pots in groups of seven on to a sheet of card. The insides of the pots can be decorated with scrunched paper, tissue or fabric. Attach these 'flower heads' to stalks made from cardboard tubes, and stand them in plastic flowerpots or decorated ice-cream tubs.

✧ Develop the children's needle and thread skills by helping them to sew 'flowers' made from colourful fabric circles on to a plain fabric background. Only one stitch per circle is needed, with the thread running across the back of the plain fabric.

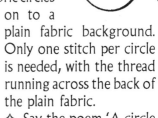

✧ Say the poem 'A circle is . . .' in the Resources section on page 71.

TURNING AND TWISTING

Objective

PE – To explore the theme of circles and spirals through body shapes and movements. To reinforce descriptive vocabulary skills.

Group size

Any size.

What you need

A room with enough space for the children to move around freely and safely, a collection of objects which roll or rotate (toys with wheels, spinning top, yo-yo, clock, paper windmill, balls, hoops, springs).

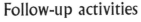

Preparation

Allow the children to handle the collection of objects. Can they share words to describe the movements of the objects — for example, spin, turn, rotate, twist, roll?

Say the poem 'Stretch, curl and twist' in the Resources section on page 67.

What to do

Use the children's observations of the objects as the basis for a movement session, and remind them of the words they used in their preparation session. Let them interpret these words using expressive body movements (twisting, spinning, rolling and so on). Invite them to use their arms and legs to change the shape of their body while they move — for example, making wide, tall, short and narrow shapes. Let the children vary the speed of their movements. Encourage them to combine any three of these actions together to create new movements — 'spinning wide and fast' or 'rolling narrow and slow'.

As the children become more confident with a range of different combinations, ask them to link two or three of these together to create a short sequence of smoothly-connected movements. Encourage them to think of a stationary pose with which to begin and end their movement sequence. Invite individual children or small groups to perform their sequence for their peers.

Discussion

Encourage the children to explain in words and actions how they hold their arms and legs to create, for example, a wide or narrow shape.

Ask the children to recall the descriptive words used during the movement session, and to remember the sequence of movements they made in response.

Follow-up activities

✧ Use the collection of words to inspire poetic language, for example: 'turn body turn', 'spin body spin', 'roll body roll'.
✧ Extend the movement session into dance by allowing the children to perform their sequence of movements in time to music.
✧ Invite the children to paint pictures of themselves and their friends dancing, spinning and twirling.
✧ Play some traditional circle games such as 'Ring-a-ring o' roses', 'The farmer's in his den' and 'In and out the dusty bluebells'.
✧ Introduce a new circle game which involves the children making up their own verses to sing. For example, to the tune of 'She'll be coming round the mountain', sing:

We are walking in a circle, you and me
We are walking in a circle, you and me
We are walking in a circle
Walking in a circle
Walking in a circle
You and me.

Encourage the children to suggest alternative actions, such as skipping in a circle, jumping, clapping, stamping, and so on.

CLOCKS AND WATCHES

Objective

History – To gain an awareness of the wheels, cogs and springs in wind-up clocks and to gain an appreciation of 'time passing'.

Group size

Individuals or small groups.

What you need

A collection of wind-up clocks (include a broken or dismantled clock).

Preparation

Show the children the mechanisms inside a wind-up type of clock. Encourage them to point out the different types of circles and spirals which make up the workings of the clock. Help them to name these parts – for example, cogs, wheels, springs. Wind the clock up and watch the different parts interact.

When the children have examined the workings of the clock, invite them to use the clock for the following investigative activities.

What to do

Ask the children to select a clock with a second hand. They can now investigate what they can do in one minute. For example:
– How many times can you draw a circle in one minute?
– How many times can you run across the playground in one minute?
– How many marbles can you count in one minute?
– How many times can you bounce a ball in one minute?
– How many times can you skip with a skipping rope in one minute?

Ask the children to record their answers in the form of numbers, words or pictures.

Discussion

Invite the children to explain their results to their peers. Can they give suggestions for alternative investigations? As they become familiar with the investigation procedure, encourage them to make predictions. For example, 'How many times could you run around the playground in two minutes?'

Talk about which activities during the day seem to pass by quickly and which seem to take a long time.

Follow-up activities

◇ Provide an opportunity for the children to find out about other types of clock: digital clocks, alarm clocks, grandfather clocks, sand timers, candle clocks, sundials, and so on.
◇ Look at your collection of wind-up clocks. What shapes are the clock faces? Ask the children to design their own clock face. Help them to add card hands that turn, using a paper-fastener.

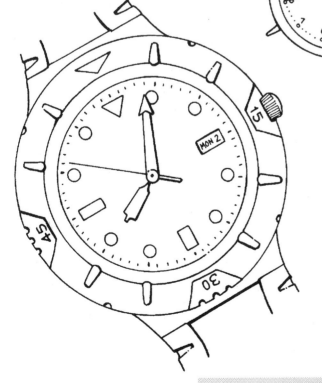

SPINNING WHEEL GREETINGS CARD

Objective

Technology – To inspire creative imagination and an awareness of basic technology.

Group size

Up to six children.

What you need

Card (approx. size A4), paper-fasteners, pens and pencils, card circles (approx. size 15cm in diameter with a hole punched through the centre), paper in different colours, scissors, adhesive, a vase of real flowers.

Preparation

Make a model spinning wheel greetings card to serve as an example for the children's work, as shown in Figure 1.

What to do

Ask the children to say the rhyme 'Ring-a-ring o' roses' while holding hands and moving around in a circle. Then show them the card you have made, with a 'ring of roses' moving around in a circle. Encourage them to take it apart and reassemble it in order to familiarise themselves with the basic technique of constructing a 'wheel card'.

Invite the children to construct their own card and to decorate the edge of the circle with a ring of colourful flowers, drawn or cut from paper. Display the real flowers nearby to inspire their imagination.

Discussion

Encourage the children to recall how they constructed their card. Can they remember the correct sequence of events?

Talk about the different sorts of card we send: 'Birthday', 'Get well', 'Thank you' and so on. Ask the children to explain who their card is for. Talk about the different messages they could put inside the cards, and help them to decide on a suitable message for their card.

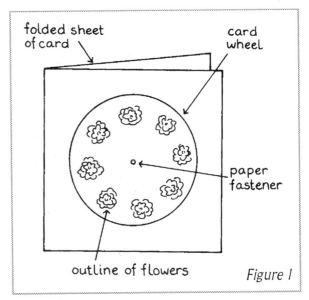

folded sheet of card

card wheel

paper fastener

outline of flowers

Figure 1

Ask the children to bring in commercial cards from home, for example birthday cards, parents' anniversary cards, cards for moving house, cards for the birth of a child and so on. Talk with the children about the different pictures and designs on the cards. Read the printed poems inside the cards and ask the children to make up their own poem or rhyme for their card.

Follow-up activities

✧ Challenge the children to use practical trial and error in designing and making an envelope for their card. Encourage them to think carefully about the shape and size necessary to fit their card.
✧ The children can design a stamp for their envelope, looking at real stamps to gain an idea of realistic shapes and sizes.
✧ Provide materials for the children to create a 'moving picture'. Some possibilities include:
– a bus with wheels which turn
– a car with a steering wheel
– a clown juggling balls.

CHAPTER 4
THREE-DIMENSIONAL SHAPES

This chapter aims to inspire children's curiosity and investigative skills. Movement activities can help the children to understand the meaning of words such as 'over', 'under', 'round' and 'through'. Activities to create number games, puppets and musical instruments can all help to develop awareness of three-dimensional objects.

ROSIE'S WALK

Objective

PE – To provide the children with an opportunity to use an obstacle course, and to give them first-hand experience of the terms 'over', 'under', 'round' and 'through'.

Group size

Small or large groups.

What you need

A hall (or, alternatively, a playground or playing field), obstacles (benches, hoops, large wooden building blocks, PE mats), the story of *Rosie's Walk* by Pat Hutchins.

Preparation

Before the children arrive, create a circular obstacle course in the hall, playground or grassed area to represent the obstructions that Rosie encountered during her farmyard walk.

Read the story *Rosie's Walk* with the children and encourage them to identify which obstacles Rosie walks 'round', 'over', 'under' and 'through'.

What to do

Invite the children to play on the obstacle course by following a series of simple instructions – for example, 'Go over one object and then go under two' or 'Go through one object, over another and around two'. Extend the activity by asking the children to take turns calling out instructions for their peers to follow.

Follow-up activities

✧ Encourage the children to recreate Rosie's walk by constructing a table-top obstacle course, using farmyard models or construction materials. Ask them to draw Rosie and the fox on two small sheets of card and then use them to re-enact scenes from the story.

✧ Help the children to devise a program for a computer toy such as a Turtle to go round objects, or to move along in a circular route.

✧ Invite the children to create a four-page zigzag book illustrating the funny events which occur as Rosie walks 'over', 'under', 'through' and 'round' the farmyard, themselves, their peers and others around them.

GREETINGS CARD

Objective

RE – To explore the theme of 'loving and giving' in terms which are relevant to the children's own lives.

Group size

The whole class can join in the preparation and discussion stages. A small group of up to four children would be appropriate for the card-making stage.

What you need

Photographs brought in by the children (for preparation work), A4 card folded in quarters, scissors, adhesive, red or pink card (approx. 4cm²), pens, pencils, crayons, felt-tipped pens.

Preparation

Ask the children to bring in photographs of people they love and who love them. Invite them to show their photographs and to talk about these special people (be sensitive to the presence of children who may have suffered the loss of a loved one). Talk with the children about how they can show the people in their photos that they love them, and how the children themselves know when they are loved and cared for.

What to do

Tell the children they are going to construct an 'I love you' card, containing a three-dimensional pop-up love heart as a special surprise.

Provide each child with a folded sheet of A4 card. Help them to cut two slits into the folded edge as shown in Figure 1, and to bend these inwards as shown in Figure 2. Then help the children to cut out a heart shape from red card and to secure it to the pop-up flap inside their card, as shown in Figure 3.

Encourage the children to use their imagination to decorate the front of their card – prompt them to think for themselves rather than imitating others.

Finally, help the children to write a message or greeting inside their card. (Some children may need an adult to scribe their message for them.)

Follow-up activities

✧ Hold an envelope-making session for the children's cards.
✧ Ask the children to design a stamp for their envelopes.
✧ Buy a stamp, then address and post a card to the school or home.
✧ Create a three-dimensional pop-up card to celebrate a religious festival (Christmas, Diwali, Eid-ul-Fitr).
✧ Tell or read the story of 'The Good Samaritan' to the children as an example of 'loving and caring' in religious terms.

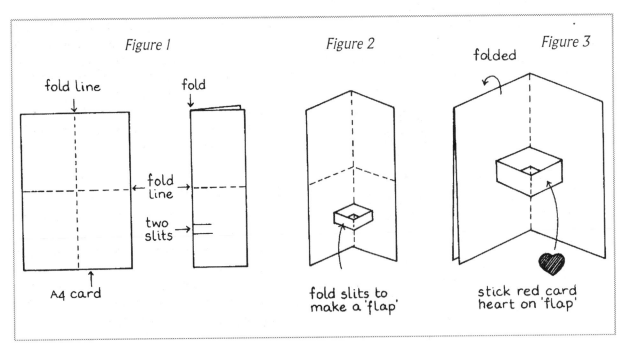

Figure 1 — fold line, fold, fold line, two slits, A4 card

Figure 2 — fold slits to make a 'flap'

Figure 3 — folded, stick red card heart on 'flap'

MAKING INSTRUMENTS

Objective

Music — To encourage an awareness of how different-shaped instruments can be made, and to investigate the range of different sounds that they can make.

Group size

Up to four children.

What you need

A selection of three-dimensional boxes, tubs, tubes, bottles and containers in a variety of shapes and sizes, card, strong adhesive tape, beads, lentils, rice, buttons, wool, fabric, paper, dowelling, long strong elastic bands, adhesive, a selection of percussion instruments.

Preparation

Allow the children to play the commercial percussion instruments. Focus their attention on the maracas, and encourage them to share ideas of how they could make their own maracas. Ask them what containers they could use. Suggestions may include:
— two yoghurt pots sealed together at either end;
— a kitchen-roll tube sealed at both ends using card, paper or fabric;
— a plastic bottle with a secure-fitting lid;
— a cardboard box with the flaps secured using strong tape;
— a margarine tub with its lid held in place using elastic bands or strong tape.

What to do

Tell the children they are going to design and make their own maracas, using a three-dimensional container and a 'filling' of their own choice. Encourage a high degree of independence during the construction stage. Let the children test the different content materials and the sounds they make before deciding what to put inside their maracas.

When the children have made their maracas, invite them to decorate these instruments using paint (on cardboard objects) or coloured sticky tape (on plastic objects).

Discussion

Discuss with the children the shapes that have been used to make their instruments. Ask them to name and identify three-dimensional shapes such as cubes and cylinders. Can the children explain how they have constructed their instruments?

Talk about the different sound each instrument makes. Ask the children to make up new names for their instruments.

Follow-up activities

✧ Let the children experiment with their instruments to help each other 'compose' original music.
✧ Help the children to record the sounds made by their instruments.
✧ The children can use their new instruments alongside others playing commercial instruments during singing or dance activities.

CLAYWORK

Objective

Art — To explore making irregular three-dimensional shapes from clay.

Group size

Up to four children.

What you need

Clay (or Plasticine or play dough), table mats or modelling boards, aprons, hand-washing facilities, a selection of irregular-shaped objects or artefacts (for example, unusually-shaped logs or stones, gourds, rocks and so on).

three-dimensional shape. Let them experiment with the clay by stretching, rolling, poking and pulling it, until they find a shape which is aesthetically pleasing from all angles.

Encourage them to decorate the surface of their shape using clay tools to give its surface texture, or using a damp sponge or wet finger to make it smooth. When it is dry, let the children paint and varnish their shape.

Discussion

Talk about the terms 'regular' and 'irregular'. Let the children handle their models while blindfolded or with their eyes shut, and encourage them to describe what they feel.

Preparation

Make sure the clay is soft and pliable enough for young hands to model. Divide the clay into small balls (the size of an adult's fist is about right).

Encourage the children to handle the objects and artefacts so as to gain an understanding of the term 'irregular shape'.

What to do

Provide each child with a ball of clay and encourage them to manipulate the whole ball into an irregular

Follow-up activities

✧ Ask the children to make a range of regular three-dimensional shapes from clay, such as spheres, cubes and cylinders.
✧ Help them to make a clay dice. This can be done by rolling a small amount of clay or Plasticine into a ball, then tapping and patting it into a cube shape. The children can then poke small holes into each 'face', using an old pen or pencil, to represent the 'dots' on a dice. When their dice are dry, let the children paint and varnish them. They can then use these dice when playing games such as Snakes and Ladders.

SHAPE PUPPET PLAYS

Objective

English – To capture the children's imagination and to inspire creative language.

Group size

Small groups of children.

What you need

For the puppets – A variety of different-shaped objects that can be used for modelling (small cardboard boxes, sponge balls, plastic bottles, paper cups, cardboard tubes, lids or trays and so on), wool, fabric pieces, felt-tipped pens, strong adhesive, adhesive tape, ribbons, lace, decorative items such as beads, buttons, shiny paper, scissors.

For the puppet theatre – a large cardboard box.

Preparation

Invite each of the children to select one of the three-dimensional shapes, and to turn it into a simple shape puppet by drawing a face on to one of its sides using felt-tipped pens and then gluing on 'clothes' made from small pieces of coloured fabric, lace, ribbon and so on. Ask them to help make a simple puppet theatre from a cardboard box with a section removed from one side, and then decorate it using paints, fabric and coloured paper.

What to do

Organise a session for the children to use their shape characters in the puppet theatre for imaginative play. Encourage them to give their three-dimensional character a name such as Cindy Cylinder, Colin Cube or Berty Box. Let the children create 'personalities' for their models during these role-play situations, for example by speaking for their character and giving him/her an unusual voice or a distinctive accent.

Encourage the children to interact in pairs or small groups in order to stimulate spontaneous stories or plays involving their 'characters'. Allow each group the opportunity to perform their 'play' for an audience. Help the children to record these stories in writing or pictures. Store the stories and plays in individual plastic wallets, and file them together to create a 'collection of works' by that group of children.

Discussion

Talk about the names of the three-dimensional shapes used for each model. Encourage the children to talk about their character and explain how they made it and what they call it.

Record the children's spontaneous stories on tape as they play with their characters. Play the tape to the children and invite them to comment on the story being told. Encourage the children to make constructive comments about each other's stories.

Share ideas about other shape characters which the children could make, for example models based on animals, fictional characters, famous people and so on.

Follow-up activities

✧ Encourage the children to make a comic-strip story about their character by dividing an A4 sheet into four or six parts. They can then illustrate a sequence of events.

✧ Compile a large story-book, written and illustrated with the children's own stories involving their models.

✧ Involve the children in making a small zigzag book (containing approximately six sections) to record the main events of their stories and plays.

✧ Set up a 'ticket office' next to the puppet theatre using a till, real or pretend money and 'tickets' made by the children. Stimulate role-play situations concerned with visiting a theatre.

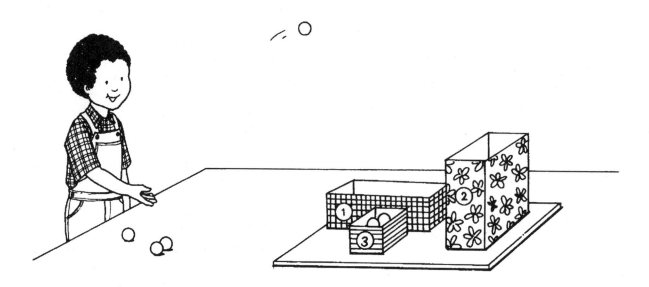

NUMBER GAME

Objective

Mathematics – To construct an educational game using three-dimensional materials. To reinforce number recognition and addition skills.

Group size

Individuals or small groups.

What you need

A selection of small boxes and cylinders, card, adhesive, small balls (such as ping-pong balls) or counters, sticky labels, pens, pencils, paints or coloured adhesive paper.

Preparation

Encourage the children to play some number games such as dominoes, snakes and ladders, number snap. Talk with them about their favourite games.

What to do

Provide each child with three to six small boxes. Ask them to stick these on to a card base in an arrangement of their own choosing.

Help the children to write a number inside each box or put pieces of paper with numbers written on them inside the boxes (the numbers should depend on the age and ability of the children). The children can decorate their game using paint or adhesive paper.

When the paint has dried, the children can try to throw two balls or counters into each of the boxes. They can then add up their total score and write it down. Let them play several times and see what is their highest score.

Discussion

Ask the children to explain how they made their game. Invite them to discuss rules and instructions for their game, and to talk about their highest and lowest scores. Discuss with the children ways of making their game easier or more complicated.

Follow-up activities

✧ Make the game more challenging by writing addition or subtraction signs next to the numbers in the boxes.
✧ Encourage the children to play their game with a friend. They can write down each other's score and compare results after each game.
✧ Invite the children to make up instructions and rules for their game.
✧ Let the children make, decorate and label a storage box for their game and its counters, rules and instructions.

INVESTIGATING SHADOWS

Objective

Science – To increase the children's awareness that solid objects cast shadows in direct light.

Group size

Individuals or small groups.

What you need

A playground or paved area, a sunny day, three familiar objects (such as a chair, a bicycle, a doll's house), chalk, a camera (optional).

Preparation

For this activity to work effectively, it is important that you choose a bright, sunny day. Immediately before the session, place three objects outside on a flat paved area where it is safe for the children to work. Draw around the shadows cast using chalk. (Alternatively, take a photograph of the shadows and complete the activity at a later date when the pictures are developed.) When the chalk outlines are complete, place the three objects in a shaded area nearby.

What to do

Invite the children outside to study the shadow drawings. Challenge them to match the objects to the correct shadows.

Repeat this activity by drawing around the same three objects when they are placed at a different angle (upside-down or facing in a different direction). Can the children still match the objects to the correct shadows? Can they work out in which position each object was placed to create the 'new' shadow?

Invite the children to draw around the shadows cast by their friends.

Discussion

Talk about the shadow shapes. Which were the easiest and most difficult to identify?

Ask the children to try to identify their peers from their shadows. If they are able to do this, encourage them to explain how, for example, pony-tails or clothing can give them clues.

Follow-up activities

✧ Mark a spot on the playground for a child to stand on, and draw around the shadow outline of the same child at hourly intervals. The children will see how the shadow has changed throughout the day.

✧ Allow the children to play at chasing their shadows. Challenge them to find out if it is possible to jump over your shadow or to run away from your shadow.

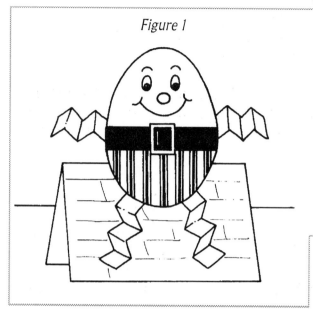

Figure 1

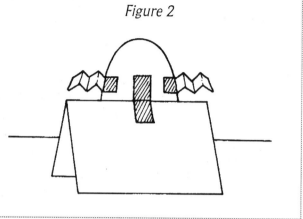

Figure 2

HUMPTY DUMPTY MODELS

Objective

Technology — To construct a tilting Humpty Dumpty on a three-dimensional free-standing wall.

Group size

Individuals or groups.

What you need

A piece of card (approx. size 15cm x 10cm) and a piece of paper (approx. size 10cm x 8cm) for each child, scissors, adhesive tape, coloured pencils, crayons or felt-tipped pens, a copy of the rhyme 'Humpty Dumpty', a template of an oval (approx. size 9cm x 7cm), four strips of paper (approx. size 1cm x 10cm each strip).

Preparation

Make your own model 'Humpty on a wall' while the children watch, to show them the basic techniques required for this activity. See Figure 1.

To make sure that Humpty can be tilted over the wall, attach him to the wall with a single strip of adhesive tape on the back only (as shown in Figure 2). He can then be tilted backwards to give the impression that he has fallen 'off' the wall. Tilting Humpty Dumpty forwards will bring him back on to the wall.

What to do

Provide each child with a piece of card to make Humpty's wall. Show them how to fold it in half so that it can stand freely, then let them decorate it to resemble a wall. Next, provide each child with a piece of paper (size 10cm x 8cm) to make Humpty's body. Invite them to draw an 'egg shape' on it or to use the oval template.

Show the children how to make Humpty's arms and legs by folding the four strips of paper to form four concertinas, two for the arms and two for the legs. Finally, help the children to bring their pieces together to create a 'Humpty Dumpty' sitting on his wall.

Discussion

Say the rhyme 'Humpty Dumpty' with the children and ask them to discuss their own experiences of falling over. Encourage them to talk about how they can help each other if one of them falls over while playing. Ask the children where they would go for help if they fell over in the playground. Use this activity as an opportunity to introduce the children to the medical room or to the person who looks after cuts and grazes.

Follow-up activities

✧ Turn the structured play area into a medical room or doctor's surgery.
✧ Compile a simple first aid kit with the children, for use in the structured play area or when anyone grazes themselves.
✧ Read the poem 'People come in all shapes and sizes' in the Resources section on page 73.
✧ Who does the poem say Humpty Dumpty looks like?

CHAPTER 5
PATTERNS

The various aspects of patterns are explored in this chapter from repeated patterns, random patterns, tessellation and symmetrical patterns to visual and sound sequences. The activities will help to foster problem-solving skills and an enthusiasm for design.

REPEATED PATTERNS

Objective

Maths — To develop the children's awareness of sequence and repeated patterns.

Group size

Small groups.

What you need

A copy of photocopiable sheet 92 for each child, a version of the story of 'The Three Little Pigs', coloured pens, pencils.

Preparation

Read the story of 'The Three Little Pigs' with the children.

What to do

Provide each child with a copy of photocopiable sheet 92. Focus their attention on the pathways linking the three piglets with their homes. Talk about the repeated patterns created by the shapes, and ask the children to identify which shapes should be used to continue each sequence. Invite the children to complete each path by drawing in the four missing shapes.

Discussion

Ask the children to look around the room to find repeated patterns; these may be found on items of clothing, curtains, carpets, wallpaper, floor tiles and so on. Encourage the children to talk about their findings and to describe the shapes and patterns seen.

Follow-up activity

Create a floor activity to reinforce sequencing. To do this, cut a selection of ten shapes from card, each approximately 10cm² in area (the types and range of shapes should depend on the age and ability of the children). Then tell the children to paint two separate pictures: a piglet and a house. When this is done, invite the children to use the card shapes to create a patterned pathway between the two pictures. They can investigate making pathways with different patterns and sequences. Develop the theme further by asking the children to work in pairs, marking out patterned pathways.

THE MAGIC CARPET

Objective

English – To inspire imagination and story-telling skills.

Group size

Small groups.

What you need

A patterned rug, felt-tipped pens, pencils, a strip of paper for each child (approx. 75cm x 20cm) folded to make a five-page zigzag book.

Preparation

Lay the rug on the floor and invite the children to sit on it. Inspire their imagination by suggesting that the rug is a 'magic carpet' which can take them anywhere they want to go. Encourage them to think of where they would like to go on their 'magic journey'.

What to do

Provide each child with a zigzag book, and tell them to use the pages to write about and/or draw an imaginary journey on a magic carpet. They should explain their adventure in the following stages (one event for each page):
– What did the magic carpet look like?
– Who sat on the magic carpet?
– Where did the journey start?
– What did they see while flying on the carpet?
– Where did the adventure end?
   The children can then give their story a title.

Discussion

Ask the children to share their ideas and fantasies about where they would go on their 'magic carpet'. Pose questions such as 'How would you command your carpet to start flying?', 'How fast would it fly?', 'What would happen if it rained or grew dark?', 'Who would you take with you on your magical journey?'

Follow-up activities

✧ Provide the children with copies of photocopiable page 93. Invite them to colour in the patterns and shapes on the 'magic carpet'.
✧ Help the children to sew a 'magic carpet' by stitching shapes cut from coloured felt on to a plain fabric background.
✧ The children can help to make a large collage depicting a magic carpet. Display this on the wall alongside the children's stories.

SIMPLE COMPOSING

Objective

Music – To introduce children to working with musical 'scores'. To develop their enthusiasm for listening to, and playing, musical instruments.

What you need

Sheets of A4 paper divided into four sections, long strips of paper (approx. size 10cm x 40cm), pens, a copy of photocopiable page 94.

Preparation

Cut up photocopiable page 94 to give four separate pictures ('hands', 'feet', 'knees' and 'mouth'), and then use the pictures to play the following game. Ask the children to sit in a circle, so that everybody can see easily; then find a place in the circle yourself, holding the four pictures face down so that the children cannot see them. Hold up the pictures one at a time. When you hold up the picture of 'hands', for example, the children should respond by clapping their hands. When you hold up the picture of 'feet', they tap their feet. The picture of 'knees' means they pat their knees, and the picture of the 'mouth' means they whistle or choose an oral sound to make. The number of times they make each sound is up to you.

Explain to the children that these pictures represent a 'code' or 'message'.

What to do

Provide each child with a sheet of A4 paper divided into four sections. Invite them to invent their own 'code' by drawing simple pictures or shapes to represent each of the four actions – clapping, tapping of feet, patting of knees and whistling. Tell them to use the sections of the paper to record the code for each action. (See Figure 1.)

Provide each child with a long strip of paper and encourage them to use their 'code' to record a sequence of actions – for example, two circles for two claps, a square for one tap of the feet, a triangle for one pat on the knees, a square for one tap of the feet and a star for one whistle (see Figure 2).

Hold a movement session in which the children ask their peers to follow their 'pattern', i.e. play their score.

Discussion

Talk with the children about their experiences of music and musical instruments. Can any of them play an instrument? What would they like to learn to play? What type of music do they listen to at home? What is their favourite song, tune or rhyme?

Follow-up activities

✧ Show the children some percussion instruments. Let them identify and name each one and investigate how they should be played.
✧ Invite the children to devise a 'code' for four of these instruments and record a musical sequence using their 'code'. The children can then play the instruments and follow their 'score'.
✧ Record these activities on tape, and play the tape back to the children.
✧ Create an interactive display featuring the children's 'codes' and 'scores' alongside the appropriate percussion instruments.

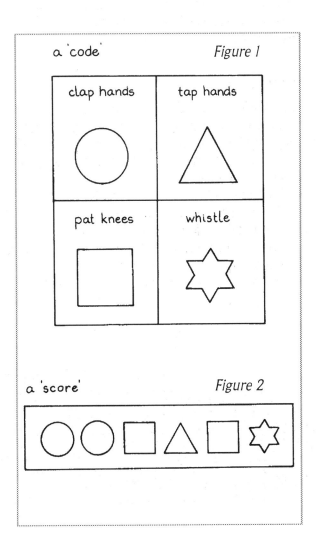

a 'code'   Figure 1

| clap hands | tap hands |
| whistle |

clap hands	tap hands
○	△
pat knees	**whistle**
□	✡

a 'score'   Figure 2

FRIENDSHIP CUSHIONS

Objective

RE – To provide a sense of belonging and stimulate an atmosphere of friendship. To create something useful which can be shared.

Group size

Any size.

What you need

Two pieces of plain fabric cut to exactly the same size (approx. 50cm²), a selection of fabric crayons/ paints and permanent colour markers, a shape template (any shape which tessellates – square, diamond, hexagon) of approx. size 12cm², masking tape, sheets of newspaper, needles and thread, pens and paper, cushion stuffing.

Preparation

Lay one of the sheets of fabric out on a table and fasten the edges down with masking tape (placing newspaper under the fabric will help to protect the table). The children could then help to mark out a patchwork pattern on the fabric using the shape template. Make sure that one shape is made on the fabric by each child in the group.

What to do

Ask one child from the group to use fabric crayons, fabric paints or a permanent marker pen to sign their name on, or decorate, one of the shapes in the patchwork pattern. Invite them to practise on a piece of paper first. When they have finished, let them choose a friend to sign or decorate one of the neighbouring shapes.

Continue this process until every child in the group has filled in one of the shapes on the fabric.

When every shape has been filled in, the children can help to sew the two pieces of fabric together and put stuffing inside to make a 'friendship' cushion for the book corner.

Discussion

Talk with the children about friends and friendship. How do they feel when they do not have a friend to play with? How do they feel when they have lots of friends to play with? How do they show that they are friends with someone?

Follow-up activities

✧ The children can contribute writing and/or drawings to a group sequence book or poster describing how they made their cushions.
✧ Read the poem 'Shapes' in the Resources section on page 72. Ask the children why they think the poem says: 'But the best shape of all is my family and me.'
✧ Encourage the children to use shape templates to create their own tessellating patterns on paper or fabric.

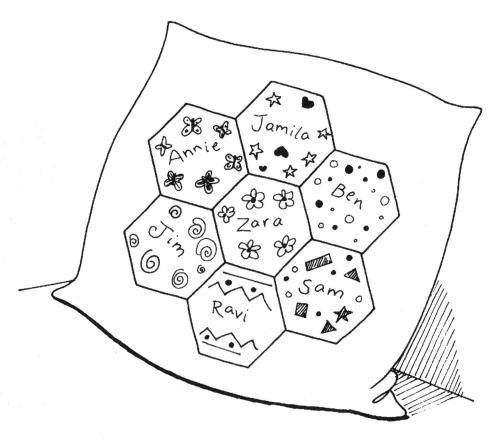

WRAPPING PAPER AND GIFT TAGS

Objective

Art – To inspire creative imagination and to widen the children's awareness of shapes and patterns.

Group size

Small groups.

What you need

Plain paper, card, paints, assorted objects that can be used to make prints, trays lined with sponge to contain paint, commercial wrapping paper.

Preparation

Look at the patterns and pictures on commercial wrapping paper with the children. Point out features such as symmetrical patterns and repeated images. Talk about the occasions when they might use wrapping paper, for example to wrap a gift for a birthday or for a religious festival such as Christmas.

What to do

Invite the children to make some wrapping paper by covering sheets of plain paper with printed patterns. Allow the children a high degree of independence in selecting their own shapes and colours to print with. Encourage them to fill all the space available.

Give each child a small shape cut from card, or help them to cut out their own shape. They can make this into a 'gift tag' by printing a pattern on to the card to match the design on their wrapping paper.

Discussion

Talk with the children about the patterns and shapes on their wrapping paper and tag. Can they recall receiving or giving someone a parcel?

Follow-up activities

✧ Ask the children to print a greetings card to match their wrapping paper and tag.
✧ The children can use their paper to wrap a small gift for someone. Help them to write on their tag and inside their card.
✧ Alternatively, mount the wrapping paper designs on the wall to create a colourful display.
✧ Turn the structured play area into a 'card shop' or 'gift shop'. The children can 'sell' their paper, cards and tags using real or pretend money. Add labels and signs such as 'Birthday cards for sale', 'Gift tags – 10p each' and 'Everybody welcome'.

DÉCOUPAGE BOXES

Objective

Technology – To demonstrate a traditional craft and to provide the children with an opportunity to make something useful.

Group size

Individuals or small groups.

What you need

Small, strong cardboard or wooden boxes with lids, magazines with colourful pictures (gardening magazines, toy magazines, comics), adhesive, scissors, varnish, a varnish brush, an old pair of child-sized gloves, aprons, hand-washing facilities.

Preparation

Prepare a small example of 'découpage' to show the children.

Introduce the term 'découpage' and explain that it is a special kind of 'cut and paste' decoration that was popular many years ago.

Encourage the children to share ideas about the different types of découpage boxes they could make: jewellery box, stationery box, treasure or trinket box, pencil box. Discuss ideas for possible patterns and designs, such as flower pictures.

What to do

Tell the children to cut out, or carefully tear, pictures of their own choice from the magazines. The subjects of the pictures are up to the children. They might all be on a similar theme, for instance flowers; or they might feature a different subject each time.

Give each child a cardboard box and invite them to open their box and then stick their pictures (in any pattern they like) on to all six outer sides, so that the whole surface is completely covered. (Make sure that the lid still opens and closes freely.) When the glue is dry, help the children to varnish their box (an old pair of gloves will protect hands from splashes of varnish).

Discussion

Talk with the children about the different patterns, shapes and designs on the boxes they have made. What will they use their box for? Is it well suited to its purpose?

Follow-up activities

✧ Suggest that the children line their box with felt or non-fraying fabric and then add a felt loop to the lid to help with opening.

✧ Encourage the children to record in words or drawings how they made their box.

✧ Use reference books to find out about the history of découpage.

INK DROP PATTERNS

Objective

Science — To discover the colours and patterns which can be made with black ink. To inspire the children's sense of investigation.

Group size

Individuals or small groups.

What you need

Black ink (or food colouring, or ink from felt-tipped pens), two pipettes, small sheets of blotting paper (approx. size 10–15cm²), water, kitchen roll, black paper.

Preparation

Inspire the children's curiosity by asking them if they think it possible to make 'pretty' patterns using only black ink.

What to do

Tell the children they are going to carry out some experiments to find out if they can make pretty patterns using black ink. Ask them to place their sheet of blotting paper on to some kitchen roll (to soak up excess dye) and then use a pipette to drip a few drops of ink or dye on to their blotting paper. Now ask them to drip water on to the dye spots. Encourage them to watch as the colours gradually separate and form interesting patterns.

When the paper is dry, help the children to mount or frame their patterns using black paper and display them on the wall to inspire discussion.

Discussion

Talk with the children about 'what they did' and 'what happened' (their method and results).

Explain that the black colour in the ink is made up of several colours mixed together.

Follow-up activities

✧ Let the children investigate colour mixing using powder paints. Challenge them to make orange using red and yellow, green using blue and yellow

and purple using red and blue. Can they make black using any combination of these colours?

✧ Use coloured dyes and small sheets of white fabric to help the children create tie and dye patterns.

✧ Encourage the children to make a written record of their 'method' and 'results'.

THE AMAZING MAZE

Objective

Geography – To use a song to inspire the children to create their own maze.

Group size

Any size.

What you need

A copy of the song 'The amazing maze' in the Resources section on page 76, a playground, chalk, pens, paper. Optional: pedal cars, bikes.

Preparation

Sing the song 'The amazing maze' with the children or read it aloud as a poem. Ask the children what they imagine this maze looks like. Discuss and compare their ideas.

What to do

Provide the children with some chalk and ask them to plan and draw a large maze on the playground. They should create three or four separate chalk 'paths' (or lines) to follow.

Remind the children of the words in the first verse of the song, to stimulate ideas for their own 'amazing maze':

Paths go here, paths go there
Paths lead people everywhere
Some paths meet, some paths part
Some paths take us right back to the start.

Help the children to make a simple 'map' or 'plan' of their maze. Encourage them to use the 'map' as they follow the paths (or lines) on foot, in pedal cars or on bicycles.

Discussion

Encourage the children to talk about their maze. Discuss the 'map' or 'plan'. Was it useful? Was it easy to understand? If not, how could they make a better 'plan' or 'map' of their maze?

Ask any children who have been in a 'real' maze to share their memories.

Follow-up activities

✧ Look at real maps. Explain that the 'maze' of lines represents real roads, railway lines, rivers and so on.
✧ Invite the children to use paints, pens or crayons to draw a maze on a large sheet of paper for a toy or teddy to solve.

CHAPTER 6
RECTANGLES AND TRIANGLES

Three- and four-sided shapes are among the most commonly-occurring shapes in our immediate environment. Learning to identify such shapes, and exploring their properties, will provide a sound basis for future learning in mathematics, science and technology.

IDENTIFYING SHAPES

Objective

Maths — To increase the children's awareness of shapes in their immediate environment. To identify and name two-dimensional shapes.

Group size

Any size.

What you need

A copy of photocopiable page 95 for each child, coloured pens and pencils, the poems 'Squares' and 'What Is a Triangle?' from the Resources section on page 69.

Preparation

Encourage the children to look at different shapes around the room, such as the shapes of the windows and doors. Send them on a 'shape hunt' to find, for example, two square objects, two triangular objects and two oblongs. Can they identify and name all of the shapes they found during their 'shape hunt'?

Read the poems 'Squares' and 'What Is a Triangle?' in the Resources section on page 69. Ask the children to identify the shapes being described. (Omit the title of each poem, as this will give away the answer!)

What to do

Provide each child with a copy of photocopiable page 95 and invite them to identify and name the different shapes that can be seen on the castle. Ask them to count the number of squares, triangles, oblongs and circles in the picture. They can then fill in each shape using the colour designated on the activity sheet.

Discussion

Talk with the children about the number of sides each shape has. Encourage them to identify objects in the room with 'three sides', 'four sides', 'five sides', 'many sides'. Invite the children to describe familiar objects within the room. Can their peers identify the object from the description given?

Follow-up activities

✧ Provide shape templates or logic blocks and invite the children to use these to create a 'Shape Castle'. Discuss the names of the shapes used.
✧ Take the children on a walk around the outside of your building to observe the variety of different-shaped windows, doors, bricks, paving slabs and so on.
✧ Introduce other shapes such as hexagons, pentagons and ovals.

ACTIVITIES

DIANA DIAMOND

Objective

English – To develop the children's listening and comprehension skills.

Group size

Any size.

What you need

The story of 'Diana Diamond's Tea Party' in the Resources section on page 86, paper (cut into the shape of a diamond – approx. size A4), coloured pens and pencils.

Preparation

Read the story 'Diana Diamond's Tea Party' to the children. Encourage them to recall events or descriptions in the story, such as the appearance of Diana Diamond's house or what happened during the 'messiest, funniest tea party'.

What to do

Provide each child with a sheet of diamond-shaped paper and ask them to draw 'Diana Diamond's house' on it. The children can choose whether it is before or after the tea party (a 'tidy' house or a 'messy' house). They must include Diana Diamond and one or more of her party guests (for example, Tracy Triangle or Sammy Square) in their picture, and draw speech bubbles next to them. The children can use their imagination to write down what each character might be saying, or an adult can scribe their ideas for them.

Discussion

Organise a session in which the children show their pictures to their peers and read the speech bubbles aloud.

Encourage the children to explain their favourite part of the story.

Follow-up activities

✧ Compile the pictures to make a diamond-shaped book, then hang it on the wall or place it in the book corner for the children to read when they want to.

✧ Invite the children to write or tell an original story about one of the other characters in the story.

✧ Ask the children to describe or illustrate the appearance of 'Sammy Square's house', 'Cynthia Circle's house' or 'Tracy Triangle's house'.

✧ Cut shapes from card and challenge the children to turn them into characters from the story.

WHERE DO I LIVE?

Objective

Geography — To motivate the children to learn and remember their home addresses.

Group size

Individuals, small groups or large groups.

What you need

Rectangles of card (approx. 10cm x 15cm), A4-sized sheets of card, adhesive, pens and pencils, marker pens, a copy of each child's home address, cereal boxes (cut open, then turned inside-out and stuck back together to create boxes with blank outside surfaces).

Preparation

Take the children on a walk in the local area. Encourage them to observe and identify the shapes and colours of front doors. What features can be found on the doors — numbers, names, doorbells, letter-boxes, windows and so on?

What to do

Once you are back indoors, provide each child with a rectangle of card (approx. size 10cm x 15cm). Let them decorate this to represent the front door of their home. When they have done this, help them to fold back the left-hand edge, then paste that edge to a sheet of A4 card, so that their 'door'

opens and closes (see Figure 1). The children can now 'open the door' and draw a picture of themselves or a member of their family behind the door (as shown in Figure 2).

Ask each child to write their name and home address in the space next to their 'door', or scribe the words for them (see Figure 3). Help them to stick this work on to the front of one of the cardboard boxes so that it stands upright, and use these models for discussion and in the follow-up activities.

Discussion

Can the children recall their own addresses? Talk about the shapes and colours of the children's front doors. What similarities are there? What differences?

Invite the children to discuss the people they have drawn behind their doors.

Follow-up activities

✧ Ask the children to use a thick marker pen to map out a pattern of two or three roads on a large sheet of card or fabric. They can place their 'front door' models on this map to create a 'toy town' of 'houses' (or blocks of flats) for their dolls, cars and teddies.

✧ Encourage the children to write a letter or draw a picture for their teddy bear or doll to send to its home on the toy town map.

✧ Invite the children to write a letter or draw a picture to send to their real home address. If possible, take the children to buy stamps for their letters and to place the letters in the post-box.

Figure 1

A4 card

door edge pasted on to card

Figure 2

door approx. size 10cm x 15cm

Figure 3

Emma Brown
3 The Road
The town
Sussex

CHEESE BISCUIT SHAPES

Objective

Technology — To provide the children with first-hand experience of mixing ingredients and making decisions regarding the shape and size of biscuits.

Group size

Individuals or small groups.

What you need

The story 'The New Baby' in the Resources section on page 81.

Ingredients: 125g plain wholemeal flour, ¼ teaspoon salt, 100g grated cheese, 75g butter, an egg.

Equipment: a mixing bowl, spoons, rolling pins, a blunt knife or shaped pastry cutter, baking trays, weighing scales, an oven, oven gloves, hand-washing facilities, clean aprons.

Preparation

Read the story 'The New Baby' to the children and talk about the different types of food made by Tom and his Gran. Can they recall the different shapes Tom used to make his biscuits, jelly and tarts?

Ask them what shapes they would choose for their own biscuits.

If the children are going to eat any of the biscuits, make sure to check whether any children have food allergies or dietary restrictions.

What to do

Make sure the children put on clean aprons and wash their hands before they begin. Involve the children in all stages of preparation.

Method

1 Sieve the flour and salt into a bowl.
2 Rub in the butter.
3 Add the grated cheese.
4 Add an egg and mix to a stiff paste (add water if necessary).
5 Roll out the mixture thinly and cut it into shapes using the pastry cutter, or encourage the children to make their own shapes using a blunt knife.
6 Place the shapes on a greased baking tray.
7 Cook at 180°C/350°F/Gas Mark 4 for approximately 8–10 minutes, or until firm and golden in colour.

Discussion

Stimulate discussion during the preparation stages as the children help to weigh, sieve and mix the ingredients. Encourage them to describe the changes in the appearance of the mixture as the ingredients are added one by one. Discuss the shapes they have chosen for their cheese biscuit.

Ask questions to draw out aspects of hygiene (Why do we wash our hands?) and safety (Why do we wear oven gloves?)

Follow-up activities

✧ Encourage the children to write about, or draw pictures to show, the sequence of events during the preparation stages. Compile this work to form a 'cheese biscuit recipe booklet'.

✧ Turn the structured play area into a café. Provide a table with cutlery, napkins and a vase of flowers, a cooking area with plates, saucepans, spoons and pretend packets of food and a service area with till, paper, pens, telephone, note-pads and so on. The children can then pretend to be waiters and waitresses, customers and chefs.

KITES WITH TAILS

Objective

Art – To develop the children's creative skills and to provide them with the opportunity to design a picture incorporating both two-dimensional and three-dimensional features.

Group size

Individuals and small groups.

What you need

Pieces of white paper or card cut into the shape of a cloud (approx. size A4), diamond shapes cut from coloured adhesive paper (approx. size 6cm x 4cm), narrow coloured ribbon (approx. length 10cm–20cm), an example of a traditional diamond-shaped commercial kite with a long tail.

Preparation

Take the children outside and help them to fly the kite. Talk about the shape of the kite, and draw their attention to the long tail fluttering in the wind below the kite.

What to do

Provide each child with a sheet of white paper or card to represent a cloud, and a selection of adhesive paper diamonds to represent kites. Invite them to stick the 'kites' on to their cloud in an arrangement of their choice. Help them to attach a ribbon to the bottom of each 'kite' and leave the ribbons dangling free to provide a three-dimensional effect.

Display the pictures on a blue background to represent the sky, and use them to promote discussion and to inspire ideas during the follow-up activities.

Discussion

Use the display of kites to reinforce mathematical expressions such as 'how many', 'count the number', 'most' and 'least'.

Talk about other four-sided shapes such as squares, rectangles and rhombuses.

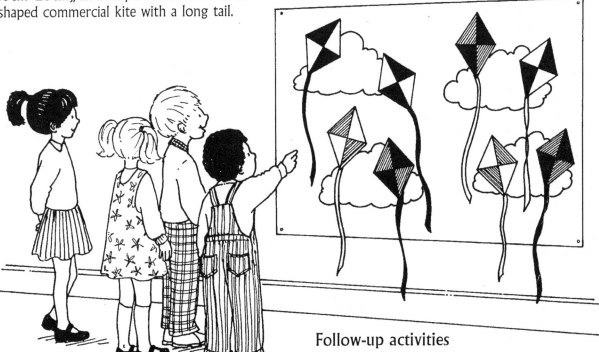

Follow-up activities

✧ Ask the children to write a story about flying up into the sky with a giant kite.

✧ Use kite-shaped templates to draw tessellating patterns on paper or fabric. Make these fabric pictures into cushions or aprons.

✧ Provide a range of craft materials for the children to use in constructing their own kite to fly outside.

✧ Sing the song 'Making Shapes' from the Resources section on page 78. Encourage the children to make up a fourth verse by substituting the word 'kite' for the word 'square'.

MEMORY WALL HANGINGS

Objective

History — To inspire interest in, and enthusiasm for finding out about, events in the past. To create a wall hanging which holds memories for the children.

Group size

Any size.

What you need

A copy of the story *The Patchwork Quilt* by Valerie Flournoy (see Recommended materials list), a triangular or rectangular template (approx. size 10cm²), colourful fabric pieces (10cm² or larger), a large piece of hessian (approx. size 40cm² or larger), fabric adhesive, dowelling, four lengths of ribbon (approx. length 15cm each).

Preparation

Read the story *The Patchwork Quilt* to the children. In the story, a young girl and her grandmother work for a year to sew a patchwork quilt. Each piece of fabric used in the quilt holds a special memory for someone in their family.

Ask the children to bring in a piece of fabric which holds a particular memory for them. Let children who are unable to bring in their own piece of fabric choose their favourite piece from the samples provided.

What to do

Invite each child to draw around the template on to their piece of fabric, then help them to cut out this shape. Help them to stick their fabric shapes on to the hessian so that the shapes fit together and leave no spaces, to make a tessellating pattern.

When the adhesive is dry, cut off the edges of the hessian, leaving a border of approximately 4cm around the tessellating pattern. The children can help to fray or hem the edges of the hessian, and to sew four loops of ribbon along the top edge. Thread a length of dowelling through the loops, so that the quilt can be hung up for display.

Discussion

Ask the children to tell you about the special memory which relates to their piece of fabric. (Children who were unable to bring fabric from home could explain why they chose a particular piece from the samples provided.) Talk about the different types of memories related to the fabric pieces — happy, funny, exciting, and so on.

Discuss other shapes which could be used to make a tessellating pattern.

Follow-up activities

◇ Encourage the children to write about or draw pictures to show the memories associated with their pieces of fabric.
◇ Help them to sew a patchwork quilt for a toy's bed.
◇ Invite the children to create a memory collage by using shapes cut from old birthday cards, gift wrapping paper, photographs, and so on.

ACTION SHAPE GAME

Objective

PE – To introduce a game which the children can adapt for their own purposes. To reinforce awareness of four-sided shapes.

Group size

Large groups.

What you need

A four-cornered room with enough space for the children to move freely and safely, four four-sided shapes (for example, kite, diamond, square, oblong) cut from sheets of card (approx. size A4), small picture cards (each illustrating one of the four shapes), a whistle, a PE mat.

Preparation

Help the children to identify and name the four shapes. Place a shape in each corner of the room in a clearly visible position. Then select one child to sit on a PE mat in the centre of the room, and place the small picture cards face down in front of that child.

What to do

Start by asking all the children to run around the room in the same direction, dodging and avoiding each other. After a short time, blow your whistle. On hearing this, the children should each select a 'shape corner' to stand in. The child in the centre then turns over one of the cards at random and calls out the shape, for example 'Kite'. All of the children standing in the 'kite corner' are then eliminated from the game and should sit down. The child in the centre shuffles the picture cards, then lays them face down again. The game continues with the children who are left. Each time the circuit begins, call out a different action for the children to follow while moving around the room: skipping, hopping or jumping. Play on until one child is left as the winner.

Discussion

Ask the children to say which is their favourite part of the game and why. Can they suggest new shapes, movements or rules for the game? Talk about other games which involve following rules or instructions: team games, party games, circle games.

Follow-up activities

✧ Ask the children to draw and cut out their own shape cards, to be used during follow-up PE sessions.
✧ Suggest that they draw or paint a large action picture to show the group playing the game.
✧ Invite a grandparent to talk to the children about games they used to play in the past. Introduce the children to some traditional outdoor games which involve co-operation and teamwork — for example, rounders or relay races.

CHANGES IN SHAPE

Objective

Science – To investigate how separate ingredients can be combined to create a loaf of bread.

Group size

Small groups.

What you need

Ingredients: 12g dried yeast, 300ml water, 500g wholemeal flour, 25g fat (lard, butter or margarine), 1 teaspoon sugar, 2 teaspoons salt.
Utensils: an oven, a jug, a large mixing bowl, a large spoon, a kneading board, a baking tin, hand-washing facilities, aprons.

What to do

Make sure the children put on clean aprons and wash their hands before they start. Involve the children in all stages of preparation.

Method

1 Mix the yeast, water and sugar in a jug, using a spoon.
2 Rub the flour, salt and fat together in a large bowl.
3 Add the yeast mixture to the large bowl and mix to a dough, using a large spoon.
4 Knead the dough. Encourage the children to change the shape of the dough by squashing, bending, twisting and stretching.
5 Place the dough in a greased baking tin.

6 Leave to stand at room temperature for about half an hour or until the dough doubles in size.
7 Bake in the top of the oven (400°F/200°C, Gas Mark 6) for 35–45 minutes.
8 Remove from the oven when baked and leave to cool. Cut the bread into slices, so the children can see how they have helped to 'change' the separate ingredients into bread.

Discussion

Encourage the children to use their own words to describe the changes in shape and texture which have occurred to the dough and the bread. Can the children recall the words used when kneading the dough – squash, bend, stretch, twist and so on?

Follow-up activities

✧ Let the children eat the bread they have helped to make (be aware of any food allergies and dietary restrictions).
✧ Investigate how other 'materials' change shape when they are warmed or cooled. For example:
i) Place ice cubes on a plate in a warm room. Encourage the children to observe what happens to the shape of the cubes as they melt.
ii) Make jelly with the children. Use warm water (not boiling) to dissolve the cubes of jelly. Let the children watch as the cubes dissolve. Place the jelly in the fridge. Point out that a fridge is a cold place. Invite the children to observe the jelly at regular intervals until it is set. Share the jelly among the children (be aware of any food allergies and dietary restrictions).

CHAPTER 7
DISPLAYS

Displays help to create a learning environment. An effective display can stimulate the children's curiosity and draw them to look closer. Wherever possible, displays should include a range of children's work – art, writing, maths, science and so on – to help them feel proud of their achievements.

The displays in our schools, nurseries and classrooms can make a statement about the learning environment. Our aim should be to ensure that this statement is positive by creating a range of quality displays. Every piece of work or poster on the walls will help to influence the visual surroundings. The leaders'/teachers' role is essential in helping children to value and appreciate their surroundings. Displays should reflect the work and efforts of the individual children, and help to promote a sense of belonging and an enthusiasm for the current topic or theme of work.

There are various different types of display, for example:

◇ displays of children's work (both 2D and 3D)
◇ interactive displays
◇ stimulus displays
◇ resource displays
◇ aesthetic displays.

Displays of children's work give the children encouragement and satisfaction. It illustrates to individuals that their work is valued and their efforts are recognised. These displays can also lift the morale of a whole class, as each child will be proud of their 'room' and feel inspired to show it off to family and visitors.

Interactive displays should openly invite children to touch, sort or use. Examples could include a 'feely table', a 'sorting table', a 'sound table' with instruments and a cassette tape, a 'magnetic table' or an 'electricity table'. Children should be encouraged to 'have a go'. Opportunities to create spontaneous pictures or writing, inspired by the display, should also be included. This work can then be stored in a 'discovery book' (a book of blank pages to be filled in by the children) or on a 'discovery board'.

Stimulus displays can be used to introduce a 'new' topic or theme. The display should consist of a main focus or attraction, plus a selection of relevant pictures, posters, information books, labels and story or rhyme books. The aim of the display should be to attract the children's interest and attention and inspire them to observe, discuss and inform. The display should also encourage the children's inquisitive nature and gain their enthusiasm.

Resource displays can be used as an ongoing, or long-term, means of storing everyday materials or tools (pens, pencils, scissors, and so on) in an interesting way. We all need to store these essential items in a practical and accessible manner, however; with a little thought and effort, they can be stored in a way that encourages the children to respect the equipment and to replace it after use.

Aesthetic displays can be used to brighten dull or dark corners, or to add small points of interest along corridors, beside doors or in hallways. These displays need not be very big, but should always be arranged with care so that they look purposeful. Examples could include flower arrangements, collections of natural objects such as shells, gnarled logs or a variety of gourds. Carefully-arranged drapes and display blocks help to create eye-catching displays.

DISPLAY 1

Based on the activity 'Symmetry shape monster' on page 26.

Display content

◇ The children's shape monster puppets (displayed on stands or boxes).
◇ The children's own stories about their puppets (made into books).
◇ Observational drawings of monster puppets (double mounted).
◇ The children's plans and designs of puppets (double mounted).
◇ Commercial stories about monsters, such as *Not Now, Bernard* and *Where the Wild Things Are*.

Decorative border suggestion

Potato print shapes could be used to decorate border strips.

Interactive label suggestions

Questions might include:
How many puppets can you see?
Find a triangle monster puppet.
Which shapes are symmetrical?

Colour scheme suggestions

A neutral colour should be used for the background. Different shades of red and yellow can be used for double mounting, the drapes, border and any labels included.

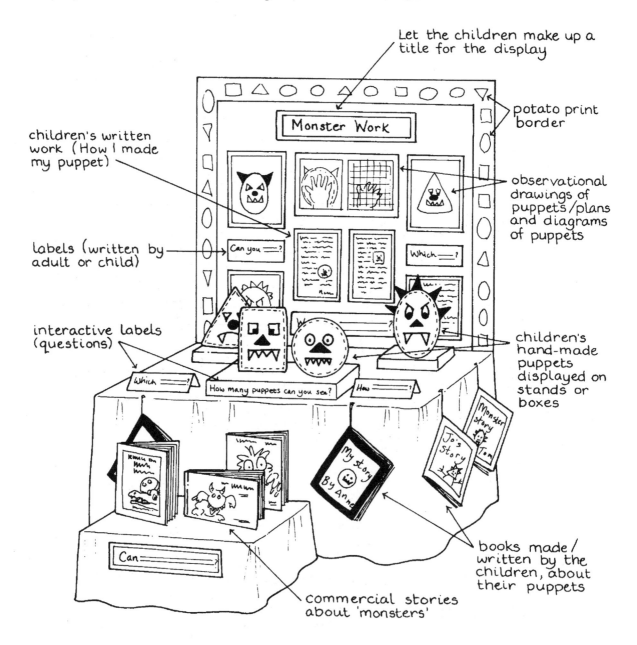

Let the children make up a title for the display

potato print border

children's written work (How I made my puppet)

observational drawings of puppets/plans and diagrams of puppets

labels (written by adult or child)

Monster Work

Can you ——?

Which ——?

interactive labels (questions)

Which ——?

How many puppets can you see?

How ——?

children's hand-made puppets displayed on stands or boxes

My story By Anne

Monster story Tom

Jo's Story

books made/ written by the children, about their puppets

Can ——

commercial stories about 'monsters'

DISPLAY 2

Based on the activity 'Kites with tails' on page 55.

Display content

◇ The children's own pictures of kites. Some can be suspended as mobiles; others can be attached to the front of cardboard boxes attached to the wall to give a three-dimensional effect. Make sure that the boxes are hidden behind the pictures.
◇ The children's own stories about being carried up into the air with their kites (double mounted on diamond-shaped paper).
◇ The children's tessellating patterns on paper.
◇ An example of a real kite.
◇ Relevant information books, picture books or stories about kites.

Decorative border suggestion

Cloud sponge prints could be used to decorate border strips.

Interactive label suggestions

Questions might include:
How many kites are there altogether?
Which is the largest kite?
In which story does the kite . . . ?
Can you find a tessellating pattern?

Colour scheme suggestion

Pale blue should be used for the background. Blue and white can be used for double mounts, the border and labels. Drapes should be in shades of purple and violet.

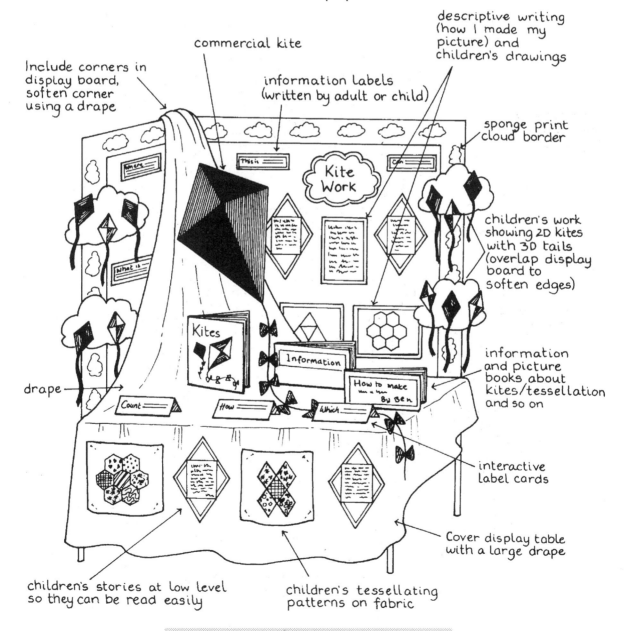

Include corners in display board, soften corner using a drape

commercial kite

information labels (written by adult or child)

descriptive writing (how I made my picture) and children's drawings

sponge print cloud border

children's work showing 2D kites with 3D tails (overlap display board to soften edges)

information and picture books about kites/tessellation and so on

interactive label cards

Cover display table with a large drape

drape

children's stories at low level so they can be read easily

children's tessellating patterns on fabric

Kite Work

Kites

Information

How to make ... By Ben

DISPLAY 3

* *

Based on the activity 'Concertina caterpillar' on page 14.

Display content

✧ The children's concertina caterpillars (on the display board, as mobiles, on fabric leaves).
✧ The children's own descriptions of real caterpillars as seen in their natural habitat and in a vivarium.
✧ The children's own stories about a 'very hungry caterpillar' (double mounted or made into books).
✧ The children's paper or fabric butterflies.
✧ Commercial stories and information books about caterpillars.
✧ A vivarium (optional).

Interactive label suggestions

Questions might include:
What does a caterpillar turn into?
How many butterflies can you see?
What colours are the butterflies?
What are the caterpillars eating in the vivarium?

Colour scheme suggestion

Blue should be used for the background, and shades of brown and green for the drapes. Decorate the background with tall 'leaves' cut from different shades of green paper. Bend and fold the leaves to give a three-dimensional effect. Double mount written work on to two shades of green. Single mount the colourful butterfly shapes on to black card.

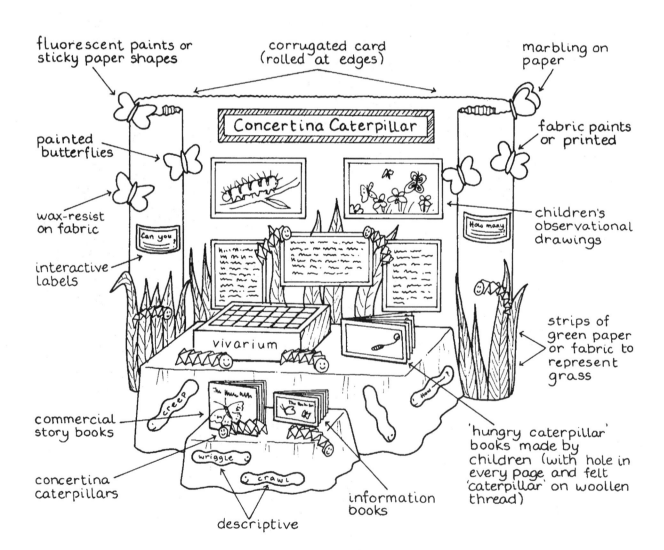

DISPLAY 4

Based on the activity 'Shape puppet plays' on page 39.

Display content

✧ A puppet theatre decorated by the children (free-standing).
✧ Three-dimensional puppets made by the children.
✧ The children's own stories and plays (made into books or placed in a folder).
✧ A ticket office (toy till, real or pretend money, child-drawn tickets).

Interactive label suggestions

Notices and questions might include:
Come and watch our plays.
Tickets for sale.
Performance daily.
Who is 'Berty Box'?

Colour scheme suggestion

Bright, cheerful colours should be used for the theatre and its curtains. Use black paper or fabric inside the theatre itself and to cover the display tables, as this will help to highlight the colours of the children's models.

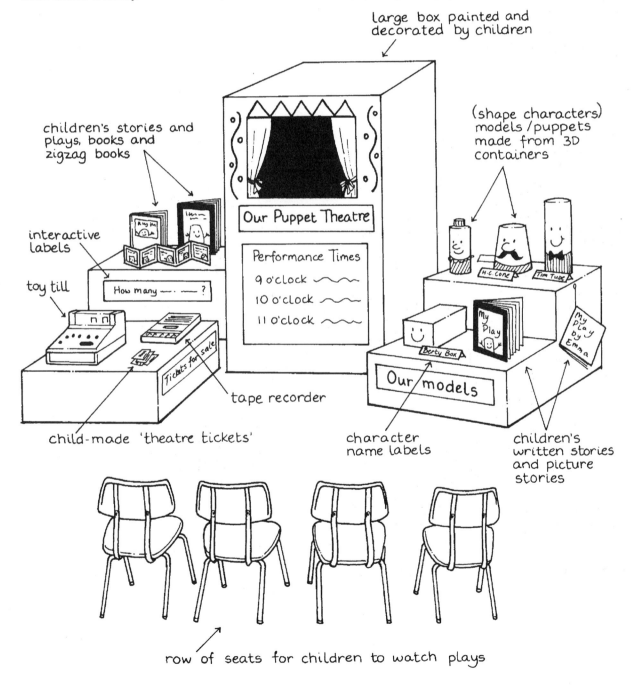

large box painted and decorated by children

children's stories and plays, books and zigzag books

interactive labels

toy till

(shape characters) models / puppets made from 3D containers

Our Puppet Theatre

Performance Times
9 o'clock
10 o'clock
11 o'clock

How many — · —— ?

H.C Cone   Tim Tube

My Play

My Play by Emma

Berty Box

Our models

Tickets for sale

tape recorder

child-made 'theatre tickets'

character name labels

children's written stories and picture stories

row of seats for children to watch plays

CHAPTER 8 ASSEMBLIES

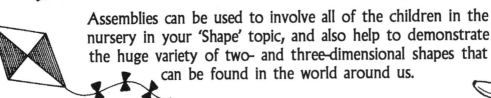

Assemblies can be used to involve all of the children in the nursery in your 'Shape' topic, and also help to demonstrate the huge variety of two- and three-dimensional shapes that can be found in the world around us.

ASSEMBLY ON BODY SHAPES

Before the assembly, hold movement activities dealing with body shapes, and choose suitable music for the children to perform to.

Introduction

Body shape can often affect self-esteem, largely due to media influences; so it is important to let children know from an early age that body shape is not in any way a token of true worth. This may be conveyed best through a humorous approach.

What to do

Cut six large pictures of people from magazines, trying to vary the body shape as much as possible. Ask six children to stand in a row facing the rest of the class, and give each one a picture to hold.

Tell the children that you are judging a contest among these six people to find which is the kindest, nicest, most friendly human being, and that they must decide the order in which the children with the pictures should stand. Can they say why their order is valid? Pose different possibilities: 'I think this person is the kindest because he has blue eyes', 'No, this person is the kindest because she has small feet', and so on. Lead the children to realise that body shape or image doesn't really tell us anything about true qualities of personality.

Invite the children to perform a movement sequence in which they change their body shapes. You will probably need to rehearse it several times, but not so much that the children become bored with their dance. Play a 'Statues' game: each time you stop the music, call out simple instructions for them to make their bodies tall, small, round, star-shaped, triangular, square, and so on. Use as many variations as you can, and include one or two that haven't been practised to add spontaneity.

Ask the children to make different shapes to represent a series of different animals which the watching children can 'guess'. Tell them to start from curled positions to become:

Hens — with puffed-out tummies and bent elbows for wings, they scurry about, then curl up again.
Cats — they stretch slowly on to hands and feet, creep slowly with arched backs, then curl up again.
Rabbits — uncurl into low crouched positions with their hands curled in front of them, move with jumping movements, then curl up again.

The children will be able to offer many others.

Settle them back down and talk about the fact that no other creatures worry about their body shapes in the way that humans do. Those creatures live their own lives, content to be themselves, and we never think twice about it. So maybe we should all be ourselves — short, tall, thin, plump . . . what does it matter, as long as we're really nice people?

Reflection

Lead the children to think about how they can stay healthy — by keeping active and fit, by eating foods that are good for them and by getting plenty of fresh air, exercise and sleep.

> **Prayer**
>
> *We thank you, Lord, for our bodies, whatever shape they are. We know it's up to us to keep them as healthy as we possibly can, and to look after them at all times. Help us to know that we must care for ourselves properly. Amen.*

Close the assembly by asking the children to think about how they can make sure they grow strong and healthy.

Song: 'I've got a body' from *Game Songs with Professor Dogg's Troupe* (A&C Black).

ASSEMBLY ON SHAPES IN NATURE

Before the assembly, make a collection (with the children's help) of natural objects and discuss their shape. The children might collect: leaves, twigs, pebbles, feathers, shells, bits of wood, grasses, flower petals, and so on. Give each child a drawn leaf to colour in, cut out and bring with them to the assembly.

Ask the children each to choose one of their favourite objects and to paint a large picture of it, focusing on its shape.

Introduction

Introduce the assembly by bringing in two identical plants, one which has been watered regularly and one which is in dire need of water. Show the children that although the two plants are the same, one is wilting because it needs to be watered. Show them, carefully, how the leaves are curling up and losing their shape. Choose a child to give a carefully measured quantity of water to the second plant. Then place both plants out of reach, and tell the children that they can look at them again at the end of the assembly.

What to do

Ask your group or class of children to show everyone their pictures of the shapes they have found in natural things. You can involve more children by appointing, for each child who shows a picture, a companion to explain to the audience what the picture shows and to describe its shape.

Explain how some of the shapes in nature are symmetrical and some are not, and have a group of children (perhaps in costume) ready to make body shapes to demonstrate this. Ask them to shape themselves into butterflies, spirals, stars, and so on. Demonstrate how a shape can be reflected by preparing a short movement sequence in which two children mirror each other's shapes.

Ask the watching children to describe the shape of a full-grown tree. Spend some time drawing the trunk and branches, with their verbal help, on a huge piece of white paper or card. When they are sure it's right, ask the children to come forward and stick their 'leaves' on to the tree using some double-sided Sellotape or Blu-tack. Ask the watching children about the shape of the tree. Does it look

about right? If the picture is of a tree in spring or summer, what might happen to it in the autumn and winter? Hang the tree picture in the background.

Suggest that the children go on their own nature 'shape' walk. Can they suggest the things they might look for?

Reflection

Encourage the children to think about how we go about our daily lives without noticing things most of the time. Perhaps they can think of ways to get better and better at observation. Looking for shapes in nature is only one of those ways. They might also look for colours, patterns, and changes in things that are affected by the weather.

Prayer

Dear God, we thank you for all the wonderful things of nature that are all around us. Most of the time we don't think about them at all, we take everything for granted. But when we really look, when we notice the circles and spheres and spirals – when we observe the real shapes and changes of nature, that's when we see real miracles. Please help us to notice miracles every day. Amen.

Close the assembly by looking again at the plant that was watered at the beginning of the assembly. Hopefully, it will have had long enough to 'pick up'. Show the children what a difference the water has made to its shape, and tell them it is our responsibility to look after the natural world and the environment.

Song: 'Watch the Stars' from *The Music Box Song Book* (BBC).

ASSEMBLY ON REGULAR SHAPES

Before the assembly make a collection of containers of all shapes and sizes, of different-shaped foods (including an assortment of shaped pastas) and of objects you can find in the home. Make a large tangram puzzle.

Take the children in your group on a 'shape' walk in the local area. Encourage them to look for and name all the different shapes they can. Help them to write or draw a record of what they find. Rehearse their contributions for the following game.

Introduction

Introduce the assembly with a game called 'On my way to school, I saw . . .' Start off by giving a shape that you saw on your way to nursery or school. For example: 'On my way to school, I saw a circle. It was the lollipop lady's sign.' Ask the children to add the things they saw. Cover as many shapes as you can. Look for the unusual – for example, a crescent might be a croissant in the local bread shop.

Prepare shape labels for the activities you intend to explore in the assembly. Let individual children be in charge of the labels until they are needed.

What to do

Give out the shape labels to the members of the audience. Place some of your three-dimensional shapes in a bag, or bags, so that the children can't see them. A child from your group or class can hold the bag while another invites individuals from the watching group to put a hand into the bag and to take out a shape, keeping their eyes closed. After feeling the shape without looking at it, the child should try to name the shape. If the child is right, the audience can give a round of applause. If the child is wrong, ask for another volunteer. Line up the shapes where they can be seen.

Each time a shape is named, ask the children to hold up their shape name labels and to choose someone to decide which label is the right one. Line up the labels with the shapes.

For two-dimensional shapes, put the children into pairs. One child in each pair holds the label. All the 'label' children sit together. The second group of children then take turns to stand up and give a definition of the shape to the watching children. For example, 'I am flat and I have three

sides that join up at points.' Invite volunteers to name the shape and to choose the matching label. The children then pair up again.

Talk about the shapes that can be seen in the room where the children are sitting; then widen the discussion to include shapes found at home, both three-dimensional and flat. Show them the collection of food and pasta and discuss the different shapes that can be found. For instance, you might have made some biscuits using pastry cutters in different shapes, a rolling pin, a pastry board, bun tins. Explain that the shape of the tools used makes a difference to the shape of the cooked food. (You might have to bake after the assembly as reinforcement!)

Reflection

Prompt the children to think about how shapes fit together. Perhaps they could investigate tessellation – when they have worked out which shapes do *not* fit together, perhaps they could do pictures of the shapes of the spaces that are left between them.

Prayer

Thank you, God, for giving us all the different shapes in the world. With shapes we can build things and fit things together. With shapes we can make patterns and pictures. Help us to use the things we know about shapes to have good ideas for all the work we do together. Amen.

Close the assembly by showing the children your tangram picture and breaking it down into individual shapes. Suggest that teachers or family might help them to make tangram pictures of their own.

Song: 'Shapes' by Jean Gilbert on page 75.

Collective worship in schools

These assemblies are suitable for use with children in nurseries and play groups, but would need to be adapted for use with pupils registered in schools. As a result of legislation enacted in 1944, 1988 and 1993, there are now specific points to be observed when developing a programme of Collective Acts of Worship in a school. Further guidance will be available from your local SACRE – Standing Advisory Council for RE.

ACTION RHYMES AND POEMS

STRETCH AND GROW

Stretch and grow, reach up high;
Stand on tip-i-toes, touch the sky!
Sink down low, down to the floor
Till no one can see you any more!

Anonymous

(Start and finish in a low, curled position, with knees on the floor, elbows and arms tucked in.)

I'M AS SMALL AS A MOUSE

I'm as small as a mouse
(Curl up small with knees on the floor and head and elbows tucked in.)
As tall as a house
(Slowly grow tall with fingertips leading the way.)
As wide as a gate
(Stretch arms wide and stand with legs wide apart.)
And as thin as a pin
(Drop arms at sides, pull in tummy and cheeks.)

Anonymous

STRETCH, CURL AND TWIST

I s-t-r-e-t-c-h
my way along a bench
As sleek as any cat,
Then I curl into a hedgehog ball
And roll across the mat.

I twist like golden leaves
That flutter gently from a tree –
Then I spoil it all by wobbling
As I balance on one knee!

Trevor Harvey

PHOTOCOPIABLE RESOURCES

POINT WITH YOUR FINGER

Point with your finger.
Point to the sky.
If you put a dot on top
You can make a letter i.

Curve your thumb and finger.
Make a letter c.
It's shaped like a banana
You can eat for your tea.
Touch your thumb with your finger.
Make a letter o.
Put it round your lips
And blow, blow, blow!

John Foster

ROLY POLY PLASTICINE

Roly poly plasticine.
What can you make?
A big fat sausage.
A flat pancake.

Roly poly plasticine.
Roll a round ring.
A necklace for a princess.
A crown for a king.

Roly poly plasticine.
What can you make?
A bendy banana.
A long thin snake.

John Foster

WHAT IS A TRIANGLE?

A pointed hat
A boat's sail flapping in the breeze.

A warning sign on the road.
A tent under some trees.

John Foster

SQUARES

The tiles on the kitchen floor.
The panes of glass in the front door.

The spaces on a snakes and ladders board.
The box by my bed where my toys are
stored.

John Foster

DRAWING A SQUARE

When you draw a square,
Take care.
Its four straight sides must be
The same size, you see.

When you draw a square,
Take care.

A square is very fair.

John Foster

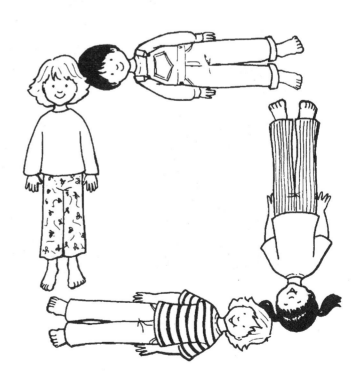

MY HAND

Here is my hand,
I can hold it out straight.

Here are my fingers
making a gate.

Here are my fingers,
watch them walk.

Here are my fingers,
watch them talk.

Here are my fingers
hiding away.

Here are my fingers
waiting to play.

Here are my fingers,
watch them run.

Here are my fingers
having some fun.

Here are my fingers
waving goodbye.

Pie Corbett

CURL AND STRETCH

Can you stand
tall as the sky?
Can you reach
way up high?

Can you curl
into a ball?
Can you curl up
really small?

Pie Corbett

A CIRCLE IS . . .

Like a hoop,
a loop the loop,
a bowl of soup.

Like an eye,
sun in the sky,
an apple pie.

Like a wheel,
a fishing reel,
a ring of steel.

Pie Corbett

STAR SHAPES

A star is a feather
from a dove's wing.
It's a silver yo-yo
bouncing on its string.

A star is a teardrop
falling down night's face.
It's a milky snowflake
patterned like lace.

A star is a jewel
in the Queen's crown.
It's a hole in the sky
to let angels look down.

Moira Andrew

SHAPES

Everything comes in different shapes
People and noses and bunches of grapes
Bugs and machinery, mountains and tyres
Vegetables, trees and smoke from fires.

Hexagons, triangles, rhombuses and rings
Rectangles and spirals make interesting things
Shapes that are square and shapes that are round
Shadows make shapes upon the ground.

Shapes that are long and shapes that are thin.
Water's the shape of the thing that it's in.
Shapes all around us up high and down low
Shapes that go fast and shapes that go slow.

Shapes on their own and shapes fitted together
Shapes that are made by people and weather.
Shapes all around us so many to see
But the best shape of all is my family and me.

Evelyn Davidson

PAVEMENT PATTERNS

Pram wheels and tyre treads
weaving to and fro
BMX and sledge tracks
skidding through the snow

Faint prints of animals
the scratch of birds' sharp claws
Ice punctured by a walking stick
the lop-sided pad of paws

All patterned in the sparkling ice
glinting in the sun
When snow dissolves to muddy slush
the street won't be such fun.

Maggie Holmes

PEOPLE COME IN ALL SHAPES AND SIZES

My grandad's head is round and bald,
It is a funny shape;
He looks like Humpty Dumpty
From his forehead to his nape!

My aunty Gwyn is tall and thin,
She stretches to the sky –
But baby Paul is pink and small
AND fat –
I wonder why?

Trevor Harvey

SCALE TALE

Triangles spread
down the dinosaur's head
and over his back
to his tail.

He walks on the land
in the mud and the sand
but each triangle
looks like a sail.

Judith Nicholls

HALL OF MIRRORS

Mirror Mirror
At the fair –
See how the people
Stop and stare
At how they look
In different guises
Of twisted shapes
And silly sizes!

Tall and stretched,
Just like elastic,
Or fat and squat
(They look 'FANTASTIC'!)

Mirror Mirror
At the fair –
See how the people
Stop and stare!

Trevor Harvey

COLLAGE

Tear the paper,
spread the peas;
snip the velvet
for the trees!

Beans and buttons,
stamps and stones;
cornflake packets,
old fish bones!

Strips of shirt
or bits of knickers,
all are used
by collage stickers!

Judith Nicholls

SONGS

SHAPES

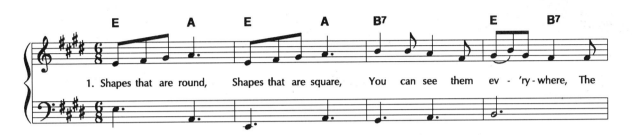

1. Shapes that are round, Shapes that are square, You can see them ev - 'ry - where, The

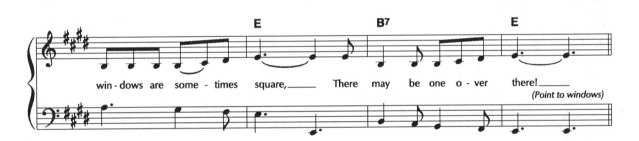

moon is round as round can be, And so is the bun you eat for tea, But

win - dows are some - times square,_____ There may be one o - ver there!_____

(Point to windows)

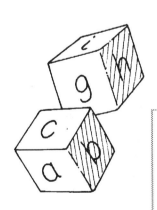

2. Shapes that are round,
Shapes that are square,
You can see them ev'rywhere.
Our building bricks are usually square,
And so are the paving stones out there,
But wheels are always round,
That's how they roll on the ground!

Jean Gilbert

THE AMAZING MAZE

Chorus

Can you guess what we did the oth - er day?____ We tried to find our way a - round the

cra - zy, cra - zy maze. In, out, round and round a - bout,

Up, down, turn a - round, a - round, What an a - maz - ing maze it is!

1. Paths go here, Paths go there, Paths lead peo - ple ev - 'ry - where.

Some paths meet, Some paths part, Some paths take us right back to the start.

Chorus

2. Now we're lost, no we're not,
Yes we are, we've had to stop.
This way's right, that way's wrong,
We've been in this maze for oh, so long!

Chorus

3. Look here's mum, dad's here too,
Hope they'll get us out, don't you?
All hold hands, make a train,
Now we're out and we can start again!

Chorus

Peter Morrell

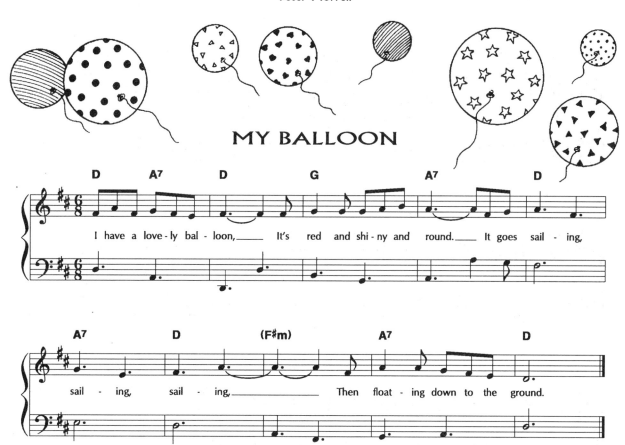

MY BALLOON

I have a love-ly bal-loon,____ It's red and shi-ny and round.____ It goes sail-ing,

sail - ing, sail - ing,_____ Then float - ing down to the ground.

Jean Gilbert

MAKING SHAPES

1. Can an-y-bo-dy here draw a square up in the air? I said Can
an-y-bo-dy here draw a square up in the air?___ De di-de di-dle di di-de
Di-de di-de di-dle di. Can an-y-bo-dy here draw a square up in the air?___

2. Can anybody sing while they're dancing in a ring? I said
Can anybody sing while they're dancing in a ring?
De di-de didle di, di-de
Di-de di-de didle di.
Can anybody sing while they're dancing in a ring?

3. Can anybody draw a triangle on the floor? I said
Can anybody draw a triangle on the floor?
De di-de didle di, di-de
Di-de di-de didle di.
Can anybody draw a triangle on the floor?

Other shapes can be substituted, for example spiral, oblong, rectangle etc.

Debbie Campbell

PHOTOCOPIABLE RESOURCES

ALLSORTS

1. Mis - ter Saus - age was long and slim. Miss - us Ball was

short and fat. Miss - us String was e - ver - so thin, *Twang!

Twang! Twang! Twang! But she did - n't care a - bout that!

*Like elastic band noises

2. Mrs Mug was empty and round
Mr Plate was round and flat
Mrs String was everso thin
But she didn't care about that!

3. Mr Tree was very big
Mrs Crocus was quite small
Mrs String was everso thin
But she didn't mind at all!

Words by Trevor Millum, music by Gill Parker

PHOTOCOPIABLE RESOURCES

CIRCLE SONG

Chorus
Walk round, hop around; *(move round in small circle: 2 steps – 2 hops – 2 steps etc.)*
Make a circle on the ground.
Stretch out 'til you feel *(touch hands in the centre of the circle)*
People's hands to make a wheel.

2. Circles in a pond, circles in the sky,
Circles in the wheels of traffic going by.
Circles you can draw, circles you can spend,
Circles when you go roller skating with a friend.

Chorus

3. Circles where you might see a tiger or a clown
Circles keep you dry when the rain is coming down.
Circles you can smell, circles you can grow,
Circles made of sand or circles made of snow.

Chorus

David Moses

STORIES

THE NEW BABY

Tom wasn't very happy about the new baby that was coming. It didn't sound as if Mum would have much time for him once it arrived.

'You'll have Somebody to play with,' Mum said. 'I'll only be in hospital for a few days. You'll be all right staying with Grandma.'

But before Tom was even half ready for it, it all happened. Right in the middle of the night. Dad woke him up and carried him out of bed to the car. 'The baby's on its way,' he said.

Gran was pleased to see him. 'We'll do a bit of cooking tomorrow,' she said.

Next day, when Tom got up, Gran was already in the kitchen.

'Your Dad will be here for his tea,' Gran said. 'We'll have a party.'

Gran got out her old glass jelly moulds. 'See these?' Gran said, holding out the moulds for Tom to see. 'You make the jelly and the blancmange and pour them in. Then, when they're set, you tip them out and you've got lovely little rabbits.'

Gran scrabbled in the cupboard under the sink for a box of plastic pastry cutters. 'These shapes make gingerbread men. And these make star-shaped biscuits. And these make teddy bear cookies.'

In the drawer she found a set of three frilly jam tart cutters – a tiny one, a medium-sized one and a big one.

They had a lovely time cooking together.

Tom made two strawberry red jelly rabbits and two raspberry pink blancmange rabbits. When they were set he tipped them out, side by side, on to a very large dish, and stuck chocolate buttons on for their eyes.

He made eight gingerbread men with raisin eyes and buttons.

He made twelve star-shaped biscuits and Gran helped him to decorate them with white icing and little silver balls.

He made six teddy bear cookies which they dusted down with icing sugar.

He made nine frilly jam tarts — three tiny ones, three medium ones and three big ones.

When all the cooking was finished, Gran put her very best round tablecloth on the table and they laid out all the food on it.

At last, Dad arrived.

He looked very pink and very excited. He picked Tom up and perched him on his shoulders and raced up and down the stairs with him. 'It's a little sister for Tom!' he shouted.

Gran said, 'Isn't she a lucky baby, to have a big brother who can do all this wonderful cooking!'

'Wow!' said Dad, when he saw the table, 'that's some party! Well done, Tom!'

When they had eaten all they could manage, they wrapped up a star biscuit, a gingerbread man, a teddy bear cookie and a medium-sized jam tart. 'We'll take a party for your Mum,' Dad said. 'She'll be very pleased.'

'And you can take a bit of blancmange rabbit to show the new baby,' Gran said. 'She won't be able to eat it, but I'm sure she'll be pleased to see what you've done.' And she gave Tom a secret little squeeze.

Mum was really pleased with the party. 'Would you mind if I ate the blancmange rabbit as well,' she said, 'after the baby's seen it?'

Tom sat on Mum's bed and cuddled up beside her. 'What do you think of your sister then, Tom?' Mum said.

He peered into the cot. So this was the Somebody to play with. She was just a teeny-weeny red-faced bundle, with her eyes closed tight together. Tom didn't know what he thought of her really.

'She's a funny shape,' he said at last.

But he must have said the right thing because everybody burst out laughing, and Mum gave him a big hug and said, 'Oh, you are lovely, Tom!'

And Tom glowed because secretly he thought his little baby sister was lovely, too.

Irene Yates

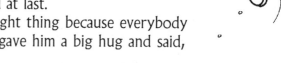

PHOTOCOPIABLE RESOURCES

THE STRANGE THING IN THE WOOD

One day, Rabbit and Squirrel were taking a walk through the wood when Rabbit suddenly tripped over something.

'Owww!' he yelled, holding his foot. He looked down and saw a silver spiral-shaped thing in the grass.

'What a strange-looking thing,' he said to Squirrel. 'What is it?'

'I don't know,' said Squirrel. 'Shall we take it to show Owl?'

Rabbit looked doubtful. 'Maybe we shouldn't touch it,' he said. 'It might be dangerous.'

'Well, you run and fetch Owl,' said Squirrel. 'And I'll stay here and guard the Strange Thing.'

As Rabbit ran through the wood to Owl's house, he told the other animals all about the Strange Thing in the wood; and of course, they all wanted to see it too. So by the time Rabbit returned with Owl, quite a crowd had gathered around the Strange Thing.

'Do you know what it is, Owl?' asked Rabbit.

Owl peered at the silver spiral-shaped thing. He walked all around it. Then he bent over it. The other animals waited with bated breath. Owl was the wisest animal in the wood. He was sure to know what the Strange Thing was.

'Oh dear,' said Owl, looking worried. 'This is very serious. Very serious indeed.'

All the other animals looked worried too.

'W-what is it, Owl?' stammered Rabbit.

'It's a tornado,' said Owl. 'It must have fallen out of the sky in the night.'

'What's a tornado?' asked Squirrel.

'A tornado is a great gust of wind that whirls across the sky, blowing everything away with it. Houses, people, animals . . . everything,' Owl told him.

The animals gasped with horror.

'Are you sure?' asked Fox. 'It looks quite harmless to me.'

'Quite sure,' said Owl. 'I have seen lots of pictures of tornados in my books. They are the same shape as this.'

The other animals quickly stepped back from the tornado and stared at it fearfully from a safe distance.

Just then, Mouse came along, carrying a bag of soft foam bits for his nest.

'What's the matter?' he asked. 'Why are you all so worried?'

'Oh Mouse, a tornado has fallen out of the sky and is fast asleep on the grass,' cried Squirrel. 'We must flee to our homes quickly before it wakes up and blows us all away!'

'I've never seen a tornado,' said Mouse. 'Let me have a look.'

'Don't touch it, Mouse!' called Owl as Mouse pushed his way to the front of the crowd.

Mouse stared down at the silver spiral-shaped thing lying on the grass and laughed.

'That isn't a tornado,' he chuckled. 'Follow me and I'll show you where it came from.'

The animals followed him, rather nervously, to a clearing in the wood. In the middle of the clearing stood an old green armchair. The arms and cushion of the chair were ripped and bits of foam were spilling out. And out of the bottom of the chair were sticking several of the silver spiral-shaped things Rabbit had found in the wood.

'They're called springs,' said Mouse. 'Humans put them in the chairs to make them more comfortable to sit on. I used to live in a factory that made chairs,' he added importantly. 'That's how I know.'

'Well, thank goodness it isn't a tornado,' said Rabbit. 'You were wrong for once, Owl.'

'And very glad I am too,' said Owl. 'Well done, Mouse!'

So the animals set off home again, all very relieved that a tornado hadn't fallen out of the sky after all.

Karen King

THE PARCEL SURPRISE

The letter from Jamie's aunty said, 'Dear Jamie, I am sending you a present. It is something that will keep changing its shape.'

What on earth could it be?

The parcel was HUGE.

It was so big it needed a van all of its own to deliver it.

It was so heavy that it took three men to lift it off the van and carry it up the path.

It was such a peculiar shape that it wouldn't go through the front door.

'Not without a bit of help,' said Dad.

So all the neighbours came round and pushed and shoved, and pulled and poked, and heaved and hoisted.

'Can't guess what's in it,' said Dad, eyeing the parcel with one eye open and one eye closed, as though something was going to jump right out and bite him.

The parcel was big and wide at one end and thin and long at the other.

'I think it must be an elephant,' Jamie said.

'It could be an elephant,' said Dad, 'But I don't think it is.'

Carefully they pulled off the first layer of paper. The parcel didn't look like an elephant shape any longer. It was big and tall and knobbly at the top.

'I think it must be a kind of a giraffe,' Jamie said.

'It could be a giraffe,' said Dad, 'but I don't think it is.'

Carefully they pulled off the second layer of paper. The parcel didn't look like a giraffe shape any longer. It was thin at the top and fat at the bottom.

'I think it must be an extremely large teddy bear,' Jamie said.

'It could be an extremely large teddy bear,' said Dad, 'but I don't think it is!'

Carefully they unwrapped the next layer of paper. Then the next. And then the next.

Each time a layer of paper came off, the parcel changed its shape. Each time it changed its shape, Jamie and Dad tried to guess what it could be.

The parcel got smaller and smaller.

It got lighter and lighter.

It got so small and so light that it would almost fit into Jamie's pocket.

'I think I know what the parcel is,' Dad said at last, stroking his chin.

'What?' Jamie whispered.

'I think,' said Dad, with a twinkle in his eye, 'I think it's really a joke! It's started off big and it's ended up small and maybe there's nothing in it at all!'

But there was. Right in the middle of all the layers of paper, there was a little cardboard box. And the box rattled.

Inside it was a shiny acorn.

Jamie was a bit disappointed. 'An acorn!' he said. 'But that doesn't change its shape, does it? Everybody knows that!'

'Ah, do they?' Dad replied. 'We'll see about that.'

He took Jamie out into the garden. They found a pot, and dug up some soil, and planted the acorn carefully in it. They put the plant pot with the acorn on a special brick at the side of the flower bed.

'Now we'll see,' said Dad. 'You just keep your eye on that acorn, Jamie — and we'll see what happens to the shape of it!'

Can you guess?

Irene Yates

DIANA DIAMOND'S TEA PARTY

In the middle of Shapetown was a big, white house. It had sparkling diamond-shaped windows, a pink diamond-shaped door and a very tidy diamond-shaped garden. It looked like the home of a very grand lady.

This is where Diana Diamond lived, and she thought she was a very grand lady indeed.

One day Diana Diamond got up very early. She had invited her friends for afternoon tea and wanted to make sure everything was spick and span.

She cleaned the house from top to bottom, and bottom to top. Then she scrubbed the garden path, picked some flowers to put in a vase and laid the table. By which time it was almost two o'clock.

'Goodness, I've only two hours to get myself ready!' thought Diana Diamond.

What a rush! First, she had a bath. Then she had to decide what perfume, shoes, gloves and jewellery to wear. That took ages.

She had just finished when the doorbell rang.

Diana opened the door and there stood Tracy Triangle, Oliver Oval, Cynthia Circle, Roger Rectangle and Sammy Square, all looking very smart.

'Oh, you do look pretty!' said Tracy Triangle. 'And what a lovely house!'

Diana was pleased.

'Do come in and I'll show you around,' she told them proudly.

She gave everyone a tour of her lovely house — then the garden — even the spotless shed! They were all very impressed.

Then she poured them each a cup of tea in her best diamond-patterned cups.

Sammy Square was hungry, as usual. 'Is it nearly tea time?' he asked.

Diana Diamond gasped in horror. She had completely forgotten all about tea. There were no cakes, no biscuits, no sandwiches . . . nothing!

PHOTOCOPIABLE RESOURCES

'I'm . . . er . . . afraid it took me so long to clean the house and get myself ready I haven't had time to make any tea,' she stammered.

'Well I never!' exclaimed Tracy Triangle.

Oliver Oval had one of his bright ideas.

'We'll help you,' he said. 'We can all make our favourite food.'

Everyone thought this was a brilliant idea.

'It's very kind of you all,' said Diana Diamond, hoping they wouldn't mess up her nice, clean kitchen.

Which, of course, they did.

Oliver Oval made some jam buns, but they looked more like jam crumbs.

Roger Rectangle tried to make an orange milkshake, but spilt most of the milk.

Tracy Triangle made her favourite chocolate cake, but turned the oven too high and burnt it.

Cynthia Circle made some peanut butter sandwiches, and covered the table with peanut butter too.

Sammy Square was so busy tasting everything, he didn't make anything except a mess.

Then everyone else started to taste the food as well, and before you knew it they were all having tea on the kitchen floor.

It was the messiest, funniest tea party anyone had ever had.

They had a lovely time, even Diana Diamond, who had always said her kitchen floor was clean enough to eat off but had never tried it before.

When everyone had gone home, Diana Diamond looked around at the pile of dirty plates, the messy stove and grubby floor, and sighed. She had spent all day cleaning the house, and just look at it!

Then she smiled. She couldn't remember when she'd had so much fun. Suddenly the mess didn't matter any more.

Still smiling, she switched off the light and did something she had never done before.

She went to bed and left the cleaning-up until morning!

Karen King

PHOTOCOPIABLE RESOURCES

THEMES
for early years

My body book 1

My body book
by
_____

Me

My body book 2

My foot

My hand

THEMES
for early years

Three bears card game

THEMES
for early years

Symmetrical patterns

THEMES
for early years

Repeated patterns

THEMES
for early years

Magic carpet

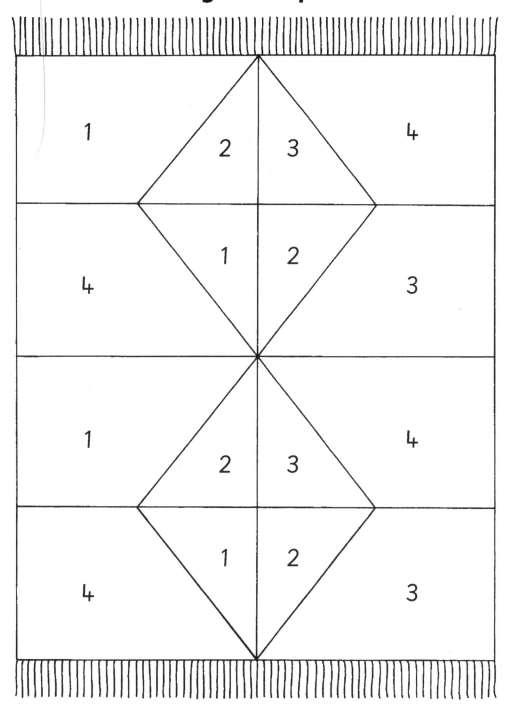

Make up your own colour code.

1 = ◯   2 = ◯   3 = ◯   4 = ◯

Colour in the carpet by following your code.

THEMES
for early years

Simple composing

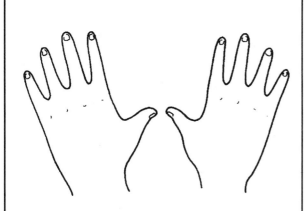

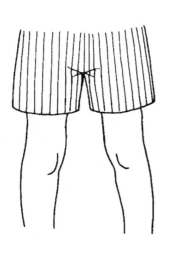

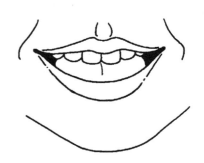

THEMES
for early years

Identifying shapes

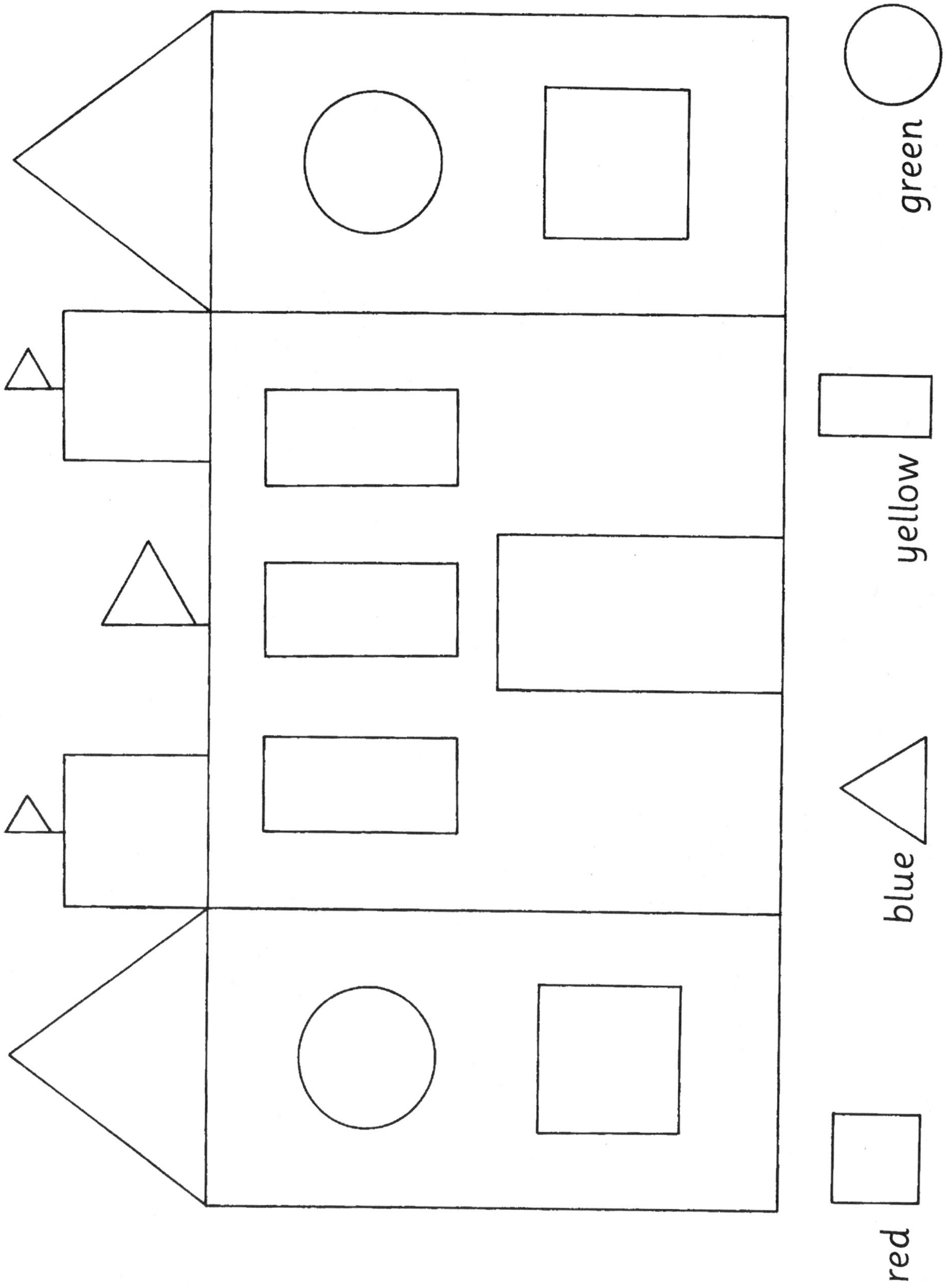

green

yellow

blue

red

RECOMMENDED MATERIALS

CHILDREN'S BOOKS

Bear Shadow F. Asch (Picture Corgi).

Baby's Catalogue J. Ahlberg and A. Ahlberg (Viking Kestrel).

Mrs Wobble the Waitress J. Ahlberg and A. Ahlberg (Viking Kestrel / Young Puffin).

Miss Brick the Builder's Baby A. Ahlberg and C. McNaughton (Viking Kestrel / Young Puffin).

Funny Bones J. Ahlberg and A. Ahlberg (Heinemann / Armada Picture Lions).

The Jolly Postman J. Ahlberg and A. Ahlberg (Heinemann).

Bears in the Night S. Berenstain and J. Berenstain (Collins).

The Snowman R. Briggs (Hamish Hamilton / Picture Puffin).

'I see a song' E. Carle (Hamish Hamilton).

The Tiny Seed E. Carle (Knight Books).

The Very Busy Spider E. Carle (Hamish Hamilton).

The Very Hungry Caterpillar E. Carle (Picture Puffin / Hamish Hamilton).

The Shape of Things D.A. Dodds (Walker).

Bears Who Went to the Seaside S. Gretz (Black).

The Patchwork Quilt V. Flournoy (Bodley Head / Picture Puffin).

Mrs Mopple's Washing Line A. Hewett (Picture Puffin).

When The Wind Blew P. Hutchins (Picture Puffin).

Clocks and More Clocks P. Hutchins (Picture Puffin).

The Doorbell Rang P. Hutchins (Bodley Head / Picture Puffin).

Rosie's Walk P. Hutchins (Bodley Head / Picture Puffin).

Titch P. Hutchins (Bodley Head / Picture Puffin).

You'll Soon Grow Into Them, Titch P. Hutchins (Bodley Head / Picture Puffin).

Not Now, Bernard D. McKee (Andersen Press / Arrow).

Sunshine J. Ormerod (Picture Puffin).

In the Night Kitchen M. Sendak (Bodley Head / Picture Lions).

Where the Wild Things Are M. Sendak (Bodley Head / Picture Puffin).

My First Nature Book A. Wilkes (Dorling Kindersley).

POETRY BOOKS

Book of Nursery Rhymes N. Bayley (Cape / Picture Puffin).

A Very First Poetry Book J. L. Foster (OUP).

Poems for 7-year-olds and Under H. Nicholl (Ed.) (Puffin).

The Puffin Book of Nursery Rhymes I. Opie and P. Opie (Puffin).

SONG AND MUSIC BOOKS

Bobby Shaftoe Clap your Hands S. Nicholls (A & C Black).

PAINTINGS

'Composition with Red, Yellow and Blue' Peter Mondrian.

'Das Lamm (The Lamb)' Paul Klee.

'Instruments of Music' Pablo Picasso.

'Twelve Sunflowers in a Vase' Vincent van Gogh.

'The Houses of Parliament – Sunset' Claude Monet.

REFERENCE BOOKS AND FURTHER READING

Simply Artistic J. Chambers and M. Hood (Belair Publications).

Display for all Seasons: a Thematic Approach to Infant Teaching J. Makoff and L. Duncan (Belair Publications).

Bright Ideas for Early Years: Favourite Themes J. Tavener (Scholastic Publications Ltd).

Young Children Learning: Talking and Thinking at Home and at School B. Tizard and M. Hughes (Fontana).

Language and Literacy in the Early Years M. R. Whitehead (Paul Chapman).

PRACTICAL RESOURCES

Shape boards: *Form Board, Shape Matching Board, Shape Sorting Board, Geo Board.* **Sets of shapes:** *Small Shape Dominoes, Magnetic Shapes, Giant Geoshapes, Soft Touch 'Clingy' Shapes, Clipy.* **Games:** *Geometrix, Place Shape, Patterns and Beads, Colour & Shape Lotto.* **Mirrors:** *Piky Mirror Games.*

All available from NES Arnold, Ludlow Hill Road, West Bridgford, Nottingham NG2 6HD.